In Mal the (handwritten inscription)

MW00583665

MANAGING
PEOPLE

THE 2020 EDITION

ERIC SWENSON

Managing People: The 2020 Edition

Published by Wheatmark®
2030 East Speedway Boulevard, Suite 106
Tucson, Arizona 85719 USA
www.wheatmark.com

ISBN: 978-1-62787-792-3
LCCN: 2020904398

Bulk ordering discounts are available through Wheatmark, Inc. For more information, email orders@wheatmark.com or call 1-888-934-0888.

CONTENTS

PREFACE

Original Preface, 2003

It was spring of 2000, and try as I might, I couldn't get a manager trainee to see the light.

Responsible for 12 managers and over 250 salespeople, my job was to get this guy to become a complete manager, as opposed to the administrator he was for almost 30 years.

It wasn't easy.

I worked with him for hours and conducted special training sessions just for him. Even though I was responsible for 20 offices, I spent 25% of my time in his office, giving advice, showing him how to be a manager — make decisions, take ownership, how to instill passion and become a visionary. At my request, he spent days observing top managers in other offices. Nothing worked. Production slipped; morale went down, he became frustrated and therefore I became frustrated.

One night, slightly discouraged and desperate for answers, I did the most mundane of chores: I went through all my computer files, deleting unnecessary ones to save disk space.

When I got to my PowerPoint files, I reviewed several presentations I'd given and seen over the years. Here were presentations on motivation, on management and on improving the process. In the course of several years, I had distilled the lessons I'd learned from other managers into these presentations, which I gave to other managers and my sales team. Some of this, I thought, would be beneficial for Mark. I took all of the presentations and consolidated it into one. There was a long outline remaining, and I started tailoring it to Mark's needs.

Late that night, I realized I had the basics of a book. Not just a specialized book on motivation, or on some specific area of management, but a general book for people who manage. I could take all the lessons I'd learned and experienced over the years, and condense into one book. And much to my surprise, the book essentially wrote itself: just one hour a night for a few months, and the core of the book was complete.

So, out of desperate concern for a manager came this book.

It sounds pretty ostentatious, doesn't it? "Managing People In the 21st Century." And just who the heck do I think I am to be able to talk about such a voluminous subject?

Especially since I am not one of those types with a Ph.D. in Business Management or an M.B.A. As a matter of fact, I did not even go to business school; I was an English major. And I certainly do not claim to be a perfect leader or manager. I made mistakes — lots of them. I've experienced failure and done things I truly regret, and sometimes I haven't always learned from my errors.

But I've been in management with two large, although completely different companies, for 17 years. I had a span of control of over 250 managers and staff, in more than twenty locations, for over six years. Prior to that, I inherited a mediocre sales team of 25 outside sales agents and took them to the top performing regional team in less than 18 months.

But most importantly, I've *been managed* by dozens of supervisors and managers — some of them excellent and some not. I paid attention to all of them, however; and always took the best elements from each of them and incorporated them into my own style.

I've attended seminar after seminar and listened to hours of tapes on management, and the one thing that is clear to me is this: you can listen to others, you can learn from others, but at the end of the day, it's up to you to perform. Not every style is for every body.

When I first started as a rookie insurance sales agent, I was 24 years old and the most significant job I ever had was as a waiter in a restaurant. I took the product training and a little bit of sales technique training, but the best thing that happened was my manager made me spend a day with each of the veteran sales agents in my office. There were 13 other agents, and I got to listen to each of their presentations, their styles and their closing techniques. I could never emulate any of them because all of us are so unique. But what I did do is take bits and pieces from each of them and incorporate them into my own style.

The same thing has happened in my management career and should apply to you as well: pay attention to each of your supervisors — whether you like them or not. You will be surprised that you will learn something from everyone. My management style is still evolving and I hope my mind is always open enough to make sure it always does evolve.

I spent several years managing managers. And the

hardest thing for me was to avoid forcing my style on managers who are struggling. The challenge is to point them in the right direction, and allow them to discover their own style.

So the concepts you are going to read about in this book are not exclusively my own. I gleefully admit to pirating from others. And you will see example after example of what I've learned—both good and bad—from the people I've worked for and with. The lessons I've learned from my own experiences in management—also both good and bad. All of these skills comprise who I am as a person, and therefore as a manager.

The opportunity to lead others is a rare challenge that has to be taken with equal doses of humility and confidence. Whether you like it or not, the person who you work for pervades your entire life. If your manager is difficult, you cannot help but take your frustrations home with you. If you have a great manager, this also affects your professional and personal life as well.

Many people want to be managers and leaders. They want the job for the power, or the money, or the authority, or whatever. The reality of managing, however, is brutally difficult at times. Not everything about leadership and management is great. When the going is the toughest is when you really earn your money. In fact, managers are not paid money to deal with the good times—they're paid to deal with problems. How well you overcome them will judge how well you succeed.

I've been blessed to work with and for some of the finest people in business today, and I hope the lessons I've learned can help you succeed as much as I have.

Author's Updates, 2020

It's semi-surreal to re-read those words seventeen years later. Essentially, an entire generation has passed. And yet, somehow, I do not feel a day older! Some people would say I do not look a day older, either.

(I paid those people.)

As I read this, the word that comes to mind is *bookends*. I spent seventeen years in corporate life, wrote *Managing People in the 21st Century*, and here we are, another seventeen years later, taking stock of what has happened and what it looks like today.

I originally wrote *Managing People* as I was exiting the corporate world. I had served my time in middle- and senior-leadership roles with two very good companies, but I was tired of being told what to do, where to be, and, especially, how to dress.

I was inspired to write the book because I thought then — and still think now — that promotions are inherently unfair. Time and time again, I watched the wrong people get promoted to management positions. They sold the most widgets, they were the most vocal in the room, they kissed the most ass. In government agencies, they even got promoted into management by passing a written examination.

But none of those things has any relationship with becoming a successful manager or leader of people.

I knew I wanted to have my own business and thought I had a niche with providing human resources, leadership, and strategic advice to small and mid-sized businesses — the same thing that the big consulting firms did, but on a smaller scale. At the age of forty, I moved in with my parents to save money and start a business without a single client in hand. I wrote *Managing People* to give myself and my future clients evidence that I could help leaders become more effective.

That was then.

Today, at the dawn of a new decade, I am fortunate and grateful to have a business with multiple brands in HR outsourcing, leadership development programs, a burgeoning practice as a leadership and workforce strategist, and a team that is incredibly dedicated and professional.

Suffice it to say, I have grown over the decades. While I got a lot right in the first edition, I got a few things wrong as well.

Despite having seventeen fewer years of experience than I do today, I actually got the fundamentals of managing people correct. The changes I am making in this edition based on our culture, economy, workforce, and workplace are really derivatives of those fundamentals. We did not have millennials in 2003, but the principles of leading them are not really different than I identified back then.

The principles of managing people are the same as ever (though it bears noting I have changed some of their names).

In the seventeen years that have passed since writing the original version, I have worked with more leaders than ever, and I have seen more businesses and learned exponentially as a result. And I have learned that I did get a few things wrong.

Perhaps it is more accurate to say that forces evolved to make those beliefs irrelevant as we enter the third decade of the millennium. Today, as I look back at some of the points I was speaking about, or writing about, or advising on just five years ago, I feel a bit as if I am revisiting the dark ages. I have updated the book accordingly.

I got the differences between leadership and management dead wrong, for instance. Back then, I believed that management and leadership are two entirely different art forms. But they are not, and I have eliminated that section entirely from this update.

I also got a lot savvier when it comes to applying concepts. Being a strategist, expert, or consultant really isn't difficult: take what you learn from one place and see if it applies to another. The hard part is in understanding what works for whom and letting go of a belief the moment it becomes obsolete.

This update reflects those insights. I ditched a few things, and I tweaked others.

This version of *Managing People* also reflects my deep gratitude.

Like many people and businesses, my business and I underwent a significant crisis in 2009-2010. The Great Recession nearly caused both of us to go bankrupt. It was an awful time. Business owners were terrified to make decisions, employees were being laid off all over the place, and we lived in a constant state of fear.

No one knew what was going to happen.

But as I wrote back then, adversity can breed success. It bred success in me, and it allowed me to concretize some of the beliefs that were only abstractions back in 2003. We came out of that crisis stronger than ever. And I learned several important lessons:

1. **Take nothing for granted.** In 2009 I was at a complete loss. I worried about making payroll. Until 2011, I

couldn't find a client to save my life. Those two years were truly life changing for me, and I'll never forget where I was.

2. **Practice gratitude daily.** The challenges I have in my business today are problems I would have only dreamed of in 2009 and 2010. How to manage our client load, keeping my team fully staffed, and choosing which clients I work with are big issues right now. They can stress me out. And then I remember where I was and where I am.

I have problems of luxury not necessity. This version represents my fortune and my gratitude.

1

HALLMARKS OF GREAT MANAGERS OF PEOPLE

1. **Communication:** Great managers are world-class communicators.

Communication has emerged as the single essential characteristic for great leaders. When I wrote the original version of this book back in 2003, it was arguably equal to the other hallmarks. Today, it is top of the list.

You can be the smartest person in the room, or the hardest worker, or the most talented, but unless you are able to effectively communicate what you want and where you want to go, then nothing else matters.

The reason great communicators often become great politicians is because they have a clear message that people understand, can follow, and can believe in.

In conducting our Tanzanite Leadership Programs, the topic I insist on teaching first is the basics of communication. Without becoming a great communicator, nothing else will help you become a great manager. We have developed 51 topics in our leadership program.

Eight of them are entirely about communication, and the other 43 involve communication to a significant degree.

That is how important communication is.

2. **Vision:** They know where they want to go and, equally important—they know how to get there.

The buzzwords of today's leadership, such as clarity and transparency, are about vision. When a leader is clear about what the goals, objectives, and expectations are, then people can help the leader get there. Over the course of conducting and interpreting countless employee surveys, I have learned that the most engaged and passionate employees are those who want to know everything that is happening within a business or organization—indeed, they feel they have *a right to know*.

A few years ago, we conducted an employee engagement survey for a long-time client, a non-profit institution in Pasadena, California, with about eighty employees. Employees were engaged and enthusiastic, but several mentioned that they wanted to know what was happening at the board level. What were the discussions? What did the future look like?

The CEO and I discussed implementing a plan to disclose certain information to employees. Obviously, many of the topics were highly confidential, but others could and should be disclosed to the employees. We decided to have the CEO write a brief e-mail after every board meeting outlining what was said and discussed.

The following year, the non-profit experienced a significant increase in employee satisfaction with respect to communication from the top.

Not every employee wants to know what is happening at the top—and that is okay. Those employees can delete the e-mail without reading it. Those employees who *do* want to know are the ones who are the most engaged, and giving them this information has a tremendously positive impact.

A vision is never a vision until we all know where we are going.

3. **Fairness:** Great managers treat employees the way they want to be treated, and they are no more demanding of others than they are of themselves.

When I wrote the original version of *Managing People,* this hallmark was called Equality. My inspiration was The Golden Rule: Do unto others as you would have them do unto you.

This concept is found throughout history and in most religions. I have quoted the rule used by Christians, which has slight variations depending on which version of the Bible is being quoted. Other versions (perhaps the original concept) can be found in Judaism, Islam, Hinduism, and Buddhism, among other religions and philosophies.

Treat others the way you want to be treated because what goes around comes around. Countless stories support this concept, but precedent to karma is the idea that treating people well is the right thing to do. Secondly, being fair is practical. I began my career working for many people who ultimately ended up working for me. Those bosses who treated me well were treated well by me in return. Those who did not? I did not mistreat them, but I doubt I was their favorite boss.

Fairness becomes even more relevant in the workplace when we start talking about diversity and inclusion, the #metoo movement, and the critical contemporary issues of equality and fairness. Great leaders of people, both now and then, recognize the many ways a person's life might be impacted by gender, race, ethnicity, socioeconomic status, background, or religion, and they strive to understand people as individuals so that they can treat them fairly, taking into account their unique and varied histories.

A corollary to "fairness" is "consistency". This is a hard concept for many employees to understand, especially if they are not top performers. Your top people should be treated differently, and it is essentially that everyone understands why. My CPA partner—the late, great Greg Snyder—was once accused of "playing favorites." When I asked him about it, he said, "Maybe those people should ask me *why* they're my favorites."

He gave me three great reasons why he played favorites.

As long as there are sound business reasons for treating people differently, and you are consistent in applying these differences, regardless of things like gender, race, socioeconomic status, and the like, then you are being consistent.

4. **Decisiveness:** Great managers can make decisions quickly and are accountable for those decisions, but they are never rigidly wed to those decisions.

In 2008, I learned about the Kolbe Theory, which was developed by Kathy Kolbe to measure and describe the specific instincts and attributes that define our natural method of operation. Some of us are Fact Finders, meaning our first action is to research. Some of us start by implementing, which means we demonstrate, produce, construct and safeguard something that already exists.

Others systematize, create the plan and bring focus and closure (which Kolbe refers to as Follow Thru).

And some of us innovate, experiment, and improvise. We are called "Quick Starts," and we deal with risk and uncertainty by making decisions—any decisions. Quick Starts experiment to see what happens and do not really worry about what the end result will be; we will figure it out and improvise along the way.

Quick Starts make decisions quickly, which is a trait I believe that lends itself to being a great manager. People want their leaders to make decisions because it shows that the leader is capable of making a decision. Employees particularly like leaders who make a decision as a follow-up of a suggestion from that employee.

Paralysis in making decisions will almost always lead to a loss of respect from your team. Get as much information as you need, involve your team in that decision-making process, understand what the result you want looks like, and go for it.

Life is too short not to make decisions, and businesses move too fast to be lost in a swamp of worries over the decision you might make. Make the best decision you can, quickly.

In the words of a very wise figure (Yoda): "Try not! Do, or do not. There is no try."

5. **Trust and Presence:** Great leaders understand the difference between being liked and being trusted.

More often these days, employees are asking for more from the people leading them. As a result, my company has worked with numerous clients and leadership program participants to discover what employees look for in leaders.

The first thing we hear is this: Employees, especially younger ones, are looking for a coach or mentor, someone who can guide them through their career. To be effective, and to have employees execute on your expectations, your employees have to trust you.

Building trust requires transparency. When you are an open book, your employers know who you are, what you will do, and whether you keep your word. The more open and transparent you can be, the more effective you will be because people can trust you.

I often speak to groups of CEOs, and I get a kick out of their reaction when I disclose the strategy younger companies are using to build transparency (and trust). These companies, often in tech, post everyone's base salary online, including those of their executives.

That is right: Everyone knows how much everyone else makes. Many old-line executives are mortified. They grew of age in an era of, "Don't ask, do not tell."

That era is long gone. Today's employees want everything above board.

This takes us to presence, the second characteristics employees ask for in great leaders. If you spend $100,000-plus to get an MBA, you will be subjected to hours upon hours of lectures about presence. I can save you the money: Act like a person you would want to work for.

We are so busy with so many things at work that it becomes easy to forget that the most important thing a people manager does is manage people.

<u>Knowledge</u>: Great leaders know their position, their industry, and what their employees do better than anyone else.

Expertise never goes out of style. One of the most frequent requests employees make of their bosses is,

"Spend time with me and understand what my day looks like every day."

This request is an important one. After all, the further away we get from being employees, the less we truly know what they are doing. This is true even if you held that job prior to becoming a manager: I promise you the job is completely different than it was when you did it.

So never forget where you came from, and be intentional about understanding what challenges your employees face.

Regarding industry knowledge: When I began my practice, I was quickly hit with an obstacle when pitching potential clients, particularly those in the banking and entertainment verticals. They asked, "What experience do you have in our industry?"

This particular obstacle was frustrating because the principles of leadership and management are not industry specific. I spent years pitching banks before I finally got one as a client. The reason they hired me? "You come to us with a fresh perspective. You are not tarnished by only working with banks."

I was lucky. That one client who took a shot on me opened the door for one of our biggest vertical markets, and now, I have a practice with many banking clients. Now, I have industry knowledge.

To enhance your credibility, proactively understand the industry you are working in. After gaining the bank as a client, I asked the executives what journals I should be reading. I went to conferences, listened to podcasts, and made myself a semi-expert on banking. That is a way to build trust.

6. **Accomplishment:** Great managers get things done.

Everyone wants to cross the finish line and celebrate a win. Doing so is essential to job satisfaction and employee engagement. When you meet those milestones, have defined moments to enjoy and celebrate them.

Dan Sullivan of Strategic Coach developed a technique that I frequently use called "The Positive Focus." The Positive Focus asks you to daily (or weekly) identify your achievements for that day or week, why these achievements were important, and what your next steps will be. We get so busy every day that we tend to forget the good things that we have done. We focus on the things we did not get done at the expense of remembering the good things that happened.

Make sure to focus on wins, not incomplete passes. Your team will have more confidence, and so will you.

7. **Style:** Great managers are never so entrenched with their professional lives to forget that a quality personal life is the most important thing to most people.

Much has been said about a so-called work-life balance. I dislike the term because it means something different to every person. Some people work sixty hours a week and think they have perfect work-life balance. Others work thirty hours and complain they do not have a life. My wife and I work really hard, but we also take meaningful vacations and trips. When I am on vacation, I am gone — completely untethered from e-mails and calls. But when I am working, I am completely in the moment. Would that work for you? Maybe, but maybe not.

Point being: Instead of work-life balance, I call it style.

Most studies show managers and executives are more engaged than rank-and-file employees; they work harder, are willing to tolerate longer commutes, and make sacrifices necessary so that their businesses (and themselves) can succeed.

It is important for managers to remember that most people work to live, not the other way around. We need to be both cognizant and respectful of our employees' time at work and away from work. Not everyone is going to want it as much as you. Once you accept that truism, you will have an easier time tolerating the employee who goes home at 5 p.m. on the dot on the evening before an urgent project is complete.

I take pride in respecting my employees' personal time. If someone is working overtime, I take it as a personal affront: I did not do a good job of planning a project or estimating deadlines. I want my people to have the flexibility to run their lives they way they want to, not how I want them to.

Not long ago, we were interviewing a candidate who said he wanted to leave his current employer for this reason: "I am getting tired of my boss calling and texting me at midnight all the time."

My operations team all smiled; they knew I would never make a midnight phone call. My longest serving, most senior team member has worked with me for nine years. In those nine years, we can count six times that I have texted her after hours. My employees might come in on a Monday morning to find a series of e-mails I have written over the weekend, but I would never invade their off-hours with a text or a phone call.

By the way, if you are the type of boss who constantly texts and calls employees after hours, shame on you. There might be an extenuating situation every once in a while, but truly, nothing is that important that requires you to do so on a consistent basis. Pestering your employees after hours shows that you are a boss who does not care about your employees, who is so self-important that every issue is earth-shaking and momentous, and who cannot control your own business. To be blunt, you do not have style.

8. **Commitment:** Great managers are committed to the success of their business unit, of the people who work for them, and of the company they work for.

Employees want to know they work for someone who is a winner, or expects to win. Further, great employees need to know that their boss has their back — that they genuinely want their people to succeed personally and professionally.

When you are distracted, it's obvious. You are always on stage. You may think you are doing a great job at hiding something, but you are not. Employees know.

I conducted an employee engagement survey for a law firm in 2014. One of the employees wrote, "I know it's going to be a good day when I hear Tony [the managing partner] humming when he walks into the office."

To put it gently, Tony is mercurial, but he was shocked people could read his mood, much less that they would notice he was humming. They knew. They always know. Commitment is like a 360-degree survey: It needs to be about you, your employees and your business. It cannot be faked; people are too smart to fall for your act.

9. **Temperament:** Great managers have level heads.

A few years after I completed the first version of this book, I joined the board of directors of a not-for-profit organization. I had no idea how dysfunctional that board was until I went to my first meeting. A couple of board members were nearly at war with the executive director over what I thought was a rather minor issue. There was little respect and even less camaraderie among the board members.

And the brand new board chair was…calm. He never lost his temper in a room where yelling and swearing was the norm. When a situation called for a time out, he called a time out and addressed the board members quietly and one-on-one. He never called anyone out in a meeting.

Slowly, the board adopted his style: disputes and disagreements were handled outside the room, allowing for course corrections by the time the board actually met as a group. Mark set a tone that others followed — either consciously or sub-consciously. It was amazing to watch, and I realized that "temperament" was indeed a characteristic of high-performing people managers.

The fact is, you cannot calm someone by giving them your own anger or frustration. This will only rile them up. And people do not think when they are flooded with emotions, so it's up to you to keep your cool and set the tone for the rest of the team.

People want to work for leaders who have a level head. It's too hard to adapt to someone who has extreme highs and lows. People respond better when a disagreement is calm rather than heated. Absent that horrible feeling of being pushed against a metaphorical wall, they are able to think reasonably, explain themselves, and change course when they gather more information.

I can recite story after story where a volatile manager had to be replaced or eliminated because people could not consistently respond well to that manager. People really do not want drama in their professional lives (most of us get enough drama in our personal lives). Of course, some people thrive on drama; those people are almost never good leaders. Temperament—the ability to maintain an even strain—is a valuable, if not essential, characteristic of great leaders.

2

WHAT IS DIFFERENT ABOUT MANAGEMENT TODAY?

Managing people in today's world requires an entirely different set of skills than it did in the past. Times change and managers have evolved and must continue to do so in order to be successful.

At the time of the Industrial Revolution in the late nineteenth century, managers were little better than slave drivers, requiring laborers to work extraordinary hours for pennies a day. Motivation (such as it was) came in the form of firing an employee. Management was autocratic and imperious (there was no reason to be anything else—no one dared question a manager). The labor force was largely un- or under-educated. Employees had no rights; there were no organized labor movements or unions, and most people felt fortunate just to have a job.

It's hard to imagine now, but at the turn of the twentieth century, it was employees who banded together to create unions. Today, the derisive term "big labor" connotes fat cat bosses smoking cigars and dabbling with pension funds. But at that time, unions were formed solely for worker safety and to negotiate a fair wage for a fair day's work. And it wouldn't be so until the 1930s, when OSHA and the Fair Labor Standards Act were enacted. Instead of dealing with employees as individuals, managers had to suddenly negotiate with them en masse—as a union. Employees received more money and had more rights, but most still felt fortunate to have a job.

The two great World Wars changed the labor market forever. With millions of men and women seconded into the armed forces, the labor market was replaced by millions of people (mostly women) who had never held a job before. Once again, managers were forced to adapt to this new type of worker. The same techniques that worked ten years before did not work now. There was no skilled labor set; these were brand new workers unaccustomed to the production line or working on a time card. Successful managers and companies adapted, but many businesses could not adapt and consequently failed.

After the Second World War, the economy became supercharged by the war-related job industries. GIs returning from years abroad had children, which created the baby boom, which continues to reverberate through society today. In the 1950s, a strong middle class appeared, and the stereotypical "nuclear family" emerged. Millions of today's executives and managers grew up in this atmosphere: Dad working 9 to 5, Mom a housewife, and 2.1 kids in school, all of them in the suburbs. In fact, the term "suburb" did not become part of the American lexicon until the mid-1950s.

In the 1980s, when I was in college, the personal computer was set to revolutionize business. I read numerous articles about how we could do twice as much in half the time. This new era was to be called "The Age of Leisure," and the big discussion was about what we were going to do with all the leisure time we would have as the computer made it so much easier to do our jobs.

Well, the opposite occurred: Instead of creating more leisure time by making workers more efficient, business moguls and owners discovered the computer would allow them to do more work with fewer workers.

There was and is no leisure time. Not in the way anyone predicted.

Today, people do more with less. They work harder for a lower quality of life than at any time in the past two hundred years. (I am not counting the upper 10 percent of society, which continues to be a leisure class as it has for decades).

Do not believe me? Think about the middle class today. How many families do you know are able to live the nuclear family lifestyle with just one breadwinner? How many people own a home, have two cars and lead a solid middle class lifestyle when only one parent works? (I do not know about you, but where I live and whom I work with, it's not a very large number).

As a consequence, there is more stress in the workplace than ever before. People believe they're working harder for a lower quality of life. And in this information age, workers are more aware of what is going on in the world than ever before. People work to live; they do not want to live to work. Only in Japan, and very few other countries, is it the other way around.

This isn't a judgment or complaint; it's a fact. It is a fact that managers must realize every day when creating their own management style. Successful managers discover what their team wants and needs, then develop a style to fit the needs of their team and themselves.

And to be sure, many employees are increasingly resistant to change in a workplace that demands constant change.

Employees look for interaction with their bosses, and the best bosses are proactive in spending some time with their direct reports. They know what questions to ask; they're great listeners, and they understand the value of those few moments they spend with employees.

Really great employees want to know what is going on in their company and feel they have earned the right to know it. This goes hand-in-hand with the need to provide transparence in the workplace.

When I was determining what a CPA firm needed to do to retain great employees, a high-potential employee told me, "I just want to listen to our managing partner have a call with our number-one client. I would love to understand what he says and what he is thinking so when I get an assignment, I have a more complete understanding of why I am doing what I am doing."

That one thing did not cost the company a dime. It increased satisfaction for the employee and created greater understanding (and more effective representation) for the firm's most important client.

3

ONE SIZE FITS ONE

I first heard this phrase in 2010 from Jonas Prising, the chair of ManpowerGroup, and it has become a mantra for me in explaining what contemporary talent management looks like even today. It accurately sums up the answer to my titular question: What is different about management today?

What is meaningful to one person is irrelevant to another, yet we continue to believe that treating everyone the same way is the right way to do something. Ridiculous! The key to effective leadership today is to discover what matters to each individual, and then find ways to mutually get to that point. Some people want to be left alone, others want frequent feedback and interaction.

I previously wrote that one of the hallmarks of great managers is that they are fair? In the original version of this book, I used equality, but the truth is, people do not want to be treated equally. They want to be treated fairly. Assuming that everyone wants to be treated the same as you would like to be treated is simply outdated.

I will use a so-called employee "benefit" story to illustrate my point.

As recently as 2010, I observed businesses invite United Way representatives into team meetings to talk about the wonderful things UW does. (They called it their "workplace giving" campaign.) The business usually offered employees the "opportunity" to donate to United Way via a payroll deduction. In fact, I observed there was often a bit of pressure applied by leaders of business to get their employees to donate.

Now, the United Way is often among the top-rated charities in the United States, and they rely on millions of passionate volunteers to help them.

But...

Not every person wants to donate to the United Way. Employees may have a favorite charity based on their life experience, or family member needs.

Today, many companies now offer employees that same payroll deduction to donate to the employees' favorite charity; it's not just limited to the United Way. Thus, one size fits one. Employees donate a higher percentage to more charities than ever today, and the individualized payroll deduction is a significant reason for that.

4

Consensus Management: What Workers and Managers Need in Today's Workplace

Because workers are more stressed and do more for less, managers cannot afford to forge an antagonistic atmosphere. Successful managers develop a style that I will call *Consensus Management*. In this style, managers encourage their employees to participate in decisions and acts that affect the entire department. Prior to making a decision, the manager has created buy-in from their team by soliciting their opinions and forging a decision by consensus.

The same theory is used at the top levels of corporate business. The successful CEO knows that an important decision isn't made at the time of a board meeting; it is made in the days and weeks prior to that meeting. The CEO solicits board members, gets input and buy-in, and by the time of the meeting, the decision is a foregone conclusion, if the CEO has a majority opinion.

Whenever I decided upon a controversial plan of action, I slowly (and individually) brought in members of my team. I laid out the problem and the situation we faced. I then outlined my potential solution and asked, "What do you think of this?"

I would take the feedback and modify my solution. Eventually, the question became: "If this is the decision, can you support this?" When I had enough people supporting the solution, I would conduct a meeting and decision was a foregone conclusion. That is consensus management.

The other benefit of soliciting feedback and asking opinions is to mitigate the shock of a change. No one likes change. Quality people learn to adapt, but no one likes it. In the summer of 2003, for example, I decided to step down from management and take a sales position with my company in order to have more time to start my own company. The decision was made in late March, but my boss asked me to keep it quiet until May. When the announcement was made to my team at a meeting, they were surprised and upset. (I cannot claim they were so devastated at my leaving as much as simply shocked at the change). It took a good two weeks of one-on-one meetings and phone calls for people to adjust to the change. Had I been allowed to "let it slip" to a few selected people, the shock would not have been as great.

Besides benefiting you as a manager, consensus management also empowers and creates a great atmosphere among your team. No one wants to be treated with disdain or a lack of respect. If I am working harder and under some amount of stress, then I would like to believe I have a say in decisions that are made by my company. I would hope my boss would consult with me from time to time on issues, or before making a decision.

One of the best questions you can ask a member of your team is "What do you think?" People want their opinions heard (and hopefully valued) — especially if an upcoming decision affects them.

So consensus management becomes the antithesis of old-style management. Old-style managers said, "Here is the way it's going to be — deal with it. And if you do not like it, here is the door." Consensus managers sound out their employees for ideas and consult with them prior to making and implementing a decision. They get buy-in. The result is happier employees who believe they are contributing to the overall good of the team.

Workers also want to be treated less as a servant class and more as equals and peers by their managers. Good team members understand and respect the person that is the boss, but they also want to know the boss cares about and respects them as individuals.

And from the opposite perspective, managers do not force their viewpoints on their employees — they treat others the way they wanted to be treated. This is an important lesson to learn — the person working for you today could be your boss down the road.

5

THE BEST BOSS YOU EVER HAD

Who is the best boss you ever had? And why was that person the best boss you ever had?

That is the question I ask at the beginning of every leadership program I have conducted over the past eight years. It brings out the characteristics of leaders most important to that person—those that truly resonate over the years.

We've tracked each response, and the five most common responses (paraphrased) are:

1. This person is transparent and a great communicator
2. This person supported me
3. This person cared about me as a person
4. This person was honest and had integrity
5. This person was trustworthy

Those are pretty good qualities in a leader, don't you think? These are overall responses, including those from millennials as well as boomers, from people just starting out in management to seasoned C-level executives.

Communication is the single most important characteristic in leadership. You can be the smartest person in the room, or the hardest worker, or the person with the most experience, but if you cannot communicate well verbally and in writing, you will never succeed.

Many younger employees use the word *"transparent"* to describe a best boss. Today's great leaders understand the need for transparency as embedded both in the organizational culture of a business, as well as a day-to-day practice of management and leadership. Communication and transparency are key to trust, in both a leader and organization.

Support means lots of things to lots of employees. My experience as a leadership and workforce strategist is that *"cared* about me as a person" and *"supported* me" are intertwined. People want a leader who will back them up and support them. The first and best way to develop that reputation is to get to know every employee as a person. If employees feel that their manager cares about them and "has their back," the employee experience is almost always going to be a positive one.

I also believe that *honesty, integrity,* and *trustworthiness* are interconnected as well. More than ever, these are essential characteristics in great leaders. Every mistake, every semi-ethical decision, is now magnified because every employee is a broadcaster, with the ability to post their thoughts (and your mistakes) on social media, Glassdoor.com, and a million other places. Doing the right thing is important, and it has never been more important than now.

Surprisingly little difference exists between what younger and older employees look for in great leaders. With all the discussions about millennials in the workplace, and their needs, it surprised me that—with rare exceptions—the same basic responses were given by young and old.

One area that showed a bit of difference is that younger employees look more for a mentor and more frequent feedback/interaction than more experienced employees. Older employees indicated their best boss was a good teacher and coach, but there is a distinct difference between a coach and a mentor.

When CEOs respond, they almost always mentioned their best boss was one who gave them freedom, regardless of how junior they were in their career. Inevitably at a leadership program, CEOs will mention their best boss "gave me enough rope to hang myself" (or some variation of that). In other words, CEOs remember their best boss was not a micromanager; trusted their good employees enough to let them make their own decisions; and gave them the freedom to work autonomously.

We work with leaders in every industry, and I can tell you the autonomous-providing-leader is pretty rare, and that is too bad: the best way to develop leaders is to remove the leash and allow them the opportunity to fail or succeed on their own. That is how CEOs become CEOs.

6

WHAT IS MANAGEMENT?

That is a pretty lofty question to ask, and one that is been asked and answered by thousands of business professors, MBAs and other students of the art of management. And you can rest assured they know a lot more about the "book end" of this question than I do. On the other hand, most of them have not worked for as many people as I have, nor managed as many! But, in deference to the bookworms, I'll amend the question to ask:

What Does Management Mean to Me?

In a sentence: successful management is simply getting your team to do what needs to be done. And — at the end of the day — it's just that simple. But the road to get there is a tricky one.

Here is what the art of management means to me:

1. Establishing Your Core Values — Identifying what is important to you professionally and personally and embodying those values every day of your life, with every action you take and every decision you make.

2. Setting and Delivering Expectations—Letting everyone around you know what:

   - They can expect from you,

   - What you expect from then, and

   - Where you want to go.

3. Communication—This is the key to everything. If you can become a master communicator, you are 90 percent of the way to being a master manager.

4. Inspecting What You Expect—It's not enough to set and communicate your objectives; you need to make sure that it gets done, and in the manner you desire.

5. Instilling Passion—To succeed, and I mean *really succeed*, you must be able to get your team to perform with passion for their jobs. And instilling that passion is only possible if you have that passion as well.

6. Taking Ownership—To gain respect as a leader, your team needs to know that all decisions are yours, even if you are just communicating upper management's wishes. It must come from you.

7. Treating People Well—The "Golden Rule" cannot be used to better effect than when you are a manager.

8. Innovate and Take Risks—I never saw a successful manager who did not take a calculated risk now and again, or who was not considered an innovator. On the other hand, I have seen many average managers

miss becoming great because they were afraid to make a mistake.

9. Adapting to Change — No one really likes change, but it is the only constant we have. Managers must be the first to embrace, and then adapt to change. Once this happens, you can get your people to embrace change as well.

10. Commitment to Success — You must be able to make a commitment to your success and that of your team. And, you have to get your team to commit to success as well. Asking for a commitment is a scary yet essential component of great managers.

11. Plan to Succeed — You cannot get where you want to go without a specific game plan, with a purpose and big thoughts.

So — that is all there is to being a successful manager! Pretty simple, huh? In the next chapters, you will learn about my philosophies on management and especially the lessons I have learned from other managers, both successful and mediocre. Remember, you can never learn enough.

7

ESTABLISHING YOUR CORE VALUES

Whether you know it or not, you have an innate set of values that you use every day in your professional life. These values guide your behavior, form the basis for your decision-making, and help define you who are— both to yourself and those around you.

I believe so strongly in creating and communicating values that I made it the core of my leadership training program, Tanzanite Leadership Development, which I spent years designing, and launched in 2019. In the first workshop, we spend two hours identifying what each person's values are. Identifying values is that important: if you do not know what you truly value, then you will never be able to decide, to take a stand. During a crisis, knowing your values makes for much easier decision making than having to re-think everything on the spot.

Much of your values come from your upbringing— your parents, your first teachers in school, and your friends. Yet your values continue to develop as you mature. I learned a great deal about myself in college and as I became an adult. I never realized at the time what I was learning. It was only in hindsight that I would recall an event or moment in my life that changed who I was forever, thus creating a core value that remained with me.

Your core values stay with you regardless of where you work, what you do, or for whom you work. They are the essence of your professional life.

Do not confuse core values with goals. Goals are much more specific and, once achieved, are over.

Most people, however, do not realize these values as a critical tool to become a top manager.

Determining Your Core Values

You already have core values—now it's time to actually identify and define them. Ask yourself:

- ✓ What do I want from my professional life?
- ✓ How do I want to be perceived?
  - ✓ From my subordinates?
  - ✓ From my peers?
  - ✓ From my superiors?
- ✓ Are these values reasonable to achieve?
- ✓ Are these values easily communicated to my superiors, my team, and myself?

Do not try to write down your core values in the middle of a hectic workday. The best time to do this is actually after a few days off, when you have had time to get away.

I've discovered—like you have—that a few days away from the job increases your perspective. It is so easy to get caught in the minutiae and routine of our job; we forget that it's our goal as managers to always keep an eye on the big picture.

Take a couple of days on vacation, then get paper and pen and write down what you want. I will give you an example of my values:

Eric Swenson's Core Professional Values

1. Make a lot of money.
2. Have a lot of fun.
3. To the extent possible, have peace and harmony in my job.
4. Conduct my business with utmost honesty and integrity.
5. Foster an atmosphere where my team believes in and shares those values.

See, that wasn't hard, was it? Those are my core professional values. What I do every day—every decision I make and every idea I have—need to have those values in mind.

In every management job I have had, I have shared those values with each member of my team. In fact, I have printed those values and framed it on my office wall. I want everyone to know what I am about and what I believe in. Then, when I make a decision, they know *why* I am doing what I am doing. And placing the values on the way ensures they know and I know why I am there—at all times.

Like everything you do, these goals will evolve, if not change, over time. One of the best bosses I had was an extremely driven taskmaster. But he always said his favorite thing to do was to teach—indeed, he was a terrific public speaker. And his goal was to get in a financial position so he could become a schoolteacher. This never would have been a value when he was younger. But when he was in his mid-40s, that became a core professional value and goal. And do you know what? He started changing. I was in sales training at the time, and he started taking a more active role in the day-to-day classroom activities, and he loved to give a special presentation or two. I hope he gets to be a teacher someday because there are a lot of young people he will truly benefit.

What Do You Want from Your Professional Life?

Volumes have been written about this, but it bears a review. Most people work to live. And I find that people who live to work often have all of their priorities out of whack.

If someone lives to work, what does that say about their individuality and their soul? Are they a person or a drone? What is the personality and where are the values they were supposed to develop over their life? And what does it mean at the end of one's life — that their big accomplishment was they worked a lot? Was it worth it?

So why do you do what you do? Do you know the answer? If you do not, you need to find out immediately, or you will most certainly suffer regret down the road.

When you examine what you want, ask yourself: Is it about money? Is it about job happiness? Is it about being close to home, or without extended business travel?

While, as a general rule, your values stay the same throughout your lifetime, what you want in your professional life will change. In 1997, I was making a reasonably good living as a sales executive. I had very high job satisfaction—a boss who left me alone; agents who were happy, driven and independent; a sales team on the rise and recognized throughout the company; and pretty good money (I worked on a commission based on how my agents produced).

By 2002, however, things were a lot different. I had a "comfortable" job, still earning close to the 1 percent. But what I did not have was freedom of time. I was being told where to be and when to be there too often. I had way too many bosses who wanted to weigh in on what I was doing (and how I was doing it). And most importantly, I was being told what to do—even down to how to dress (Business suit—not even a coat-and tie!). I turned forty that year, and I got tired of being told what to do.

Thus, freedom of time (and management bureaucracy) was more important than comfort. My choice was either get out then, or stay frustrated for the next 25 years. I chose the former.

How Do You Want to Be Perceived by Your Subordinates, Peers, and Superiors?

Some people glibly say, "I do not care what anyone else thinks of me. I am going to do what I want to do." But once you get into management, *how* you want to be perceived and how you *are* perceived are both especially important, especially as they pertain to your subordinates. You—and you alone—affect that perception.

(Beyond that, we are hardwired to want people to like us. Brené Brown says this of people who do not care what others think of them: "That is the very definition of a psychopath!")

Successful management means you are secure enough with your own values and beliefs to minimize the problems people create for you in your job because you are satisfied in your own personal and social life.

I once worked for an executive who loved addressing every new training class. One of his favorite sayings was, "We want you working hard between 8 a.m. and 5 p.m., occasionally to 6 p.m., but we do not want you working late at night or on weekends because we believe if you have a great home life and a great social life, you will have a great business life." He was dead on.

Successful management also means that you must set a path of what you think is right. What is right is not always popular. You either read polls and act (the definition of a follower), or you will decide what you think is the best and right course of action (the definition of a leader). Of course, you should solicit the opinions of others (consensus management), but ultimately leaders must act in a way true to their values and beliefs.

A while ago, I sat in on a verbal counseling with a sales representative who had been highly successful the year before, but whose recent production had been below average and well below quota. Her manager asked me to witness the meeting. The rep was shaking as she walked in.

The manager said, "Penny, we are here to discuss your production. Eric and I need to understand what is going on. Your recent production is unlike you. What is happening?"

The rep started talking about how hard she was working, but something did not ring true with me. I decided to interject.

"Penny, what is really going on? Something traumatic must have happened for this to be happening to you."

And out came the tears. Turns out Penny had

suffered several family tragedies and setbacks in the past few months. Her manager and I discussed with her the most intimate and private details of her life, and it was difficult for everyone. Penny was upset, especially when I had to re-focus the discussion back on business. She was clearly distressed with me and said so. But I had a business to run: I needed her to work through her problems and succeed, or give up and punt. That is what we talked about.

I do not regret getting her so mad because as a manager my responsibility was running a successful business. The rep either needed to resolve her problems and continue producing, or not. I recommended counseling as a way of solving those problems. In any instance, the rep disliked me intensely. It did not matter to me — I was there for two reasons, and I wanted to be perceived as being there for those two reasons: to help a fellow employee, and ensure our success as a team. The last thing I needed was to worry if Penny liked me or not.

But I did need to care about how I was perceived. For me, I want everyone to know that I want to win. I want to be associated with winners, and I want to win through playing by the rules. Once I became a successful manager, I enjoyed attending corporate trips and conferences in exotic locations with my top salespeople. At corporate meetings, I tended to sit with them.

My boss finally noticed this and told me, "Your biggest problem is that you hang out only with your top people and do not spend enough time with your mediocre people."

He was right—I do not want to hang out around people who do not have or commit to the same success that I do.

Therein lies one of the biggest paradoxes of management: Not everyone who works for you is going to have the drive you do. I recently talked with Debbie, who got promoted into management on the basis of a spectacular five-year career in sales. Her biggest frustration in her new job was exactly that—not everyone was as driven as she was.

That is natural—and that is why Debbie got promoted into management—top management recognizes (or should, at least) those who are driven to succeed and tend to promote those people into management and beyond. There is no solution to Debbie's dilemma, either—I told her that dozens of managers I have worked with (including myself) have felt that frustration. There are some techniques in this book that can help instill passion in people—but the bottom line is—not everyone is as driven to succeed as you are, and you either need to accept and work with that fact, or find people who do.

I will never tolerate—in an employee or myself—any unethical or untoward behavior. Winning at all costs does not work with me. Winning the right way is the only way to win.

So how do you want to be perceived by your employees? As a tough but fair leader? As a compassionate, caring colleague? Your actions—and your core values— will guide you in making this decision.

If your employees know what you are about—then they will always be more understanding of your style.

Are These Values Aggressive but Reasonable?

Nothing is wrong with aiming high. That is what goals are for, not values. Be really careful with confusing core values and goals.

Here is a goal: "I want to be CEO."

Here is a value: "I want to conduct my business and lead my team to ensure everyone maximizes their potential and therefore we all succeed."

See the difference? Goals are specific, and values are the way you conduct yourself. If you follow the values you establish, you will ultimately find promotion and success.

I have worked for only two companies since college. Trying to get a sales job as my first position was difficult, to say the least. I had moved back home from college in 1986, and I had interviewed for a number of jobs but not successfully. In fact, I had interviewed at one company for several positions that paid less than the job they finally offered me.

Then one day in October, I got a call to interview with a manager in Long Beach. The position was insurance agent. I introduced myself and handed him my *résumé*. He reviewed it, then dropped the *résumé,* looked up to me, and said, "You are an Eagle Scout."

I acknowledged that I was, and he said, "When can you start?"

(Right away, as it turned out). There was never any interview.

Several years later, I got the gumption to ask him what it was about an Eagle Scout that made him hire me on the spot. He told me that although he never was an Eagle Scout, two of his sons were. And if my values and drive were good enough to become an Eagle Scout, they were good enough for him. He had identified those values as important to him as well.

That was a nice compliment to me. And the critical lesson I learned was this: You cannot shoot too high when establishing your core values. Set standards that are lofty, aggressive, and a little scary—but that you can achieve.

Are These Values Easily Communicated to Yourself, Your Superior, and Your Team?

For heaven's sake, do not write a novel when establishing your core values. Each value should only be one sentence. You want people to read, understand, and buy-in to your values, not look at a 5,000-word treatise and fall asleep.

Your values should consist of one sentence each and fit on one piece of paper that I strongly recommend placing in a highly visible spot in your office. You want your people to be reminded of your values every day. And the most important person that needs to be reminded is you.

It is also important that your immediate superior see your core values. Hopefully in hiring you, he or she knows something of those values already. But it is an excellent idea to share it with your boss. I am sure your boss knew something of your values prior to hiring or promoting you, but an important meeting takes place when you sit him or her down and only talk about your values.

One of my favorite employees, Terry, was a manager and infamous as a loose cannon. She had no fear of telling it as she saw it, to the chagrin of many executives, but I liked Terry's candor. She told me what she thought, and I appreciated hearing candid and non-filtered opinions.

Terry challenged a number of my decisions and ideas, and eventually it started driving me crazy. Then one day at lunch, we talked about what her values were. It turned out that her most important values were integrity, quality, and success. I realized then that her feistiness was due to her core values — if something or someone were not up to her standards, then she created a scene.

What an insight! I was then able to frame my suggestions and discussions in the context of quality — or, if I had to deliver bad news, I was able to frame my arguments to include the need for integrity and quality.

As a manager of managers, I had no desire to know all the detailed stuff each one did. But what does interest me is the foundation they set for their management style and beliefs. That foundation shows how we can plan to accomplish the goals we mutually set for each other.

8

SETTING AND DELIVERING EXPECTATIONS

There isn't a more important duty of a manager than letting your employees know precisely what you expect of them. A good analogy is related to parents of a young child. A toddler has and needs parameters and guidelines — slip over the line, and here comes the punishment!

Even a puppy has expectations. A puppy knows it can and cannot do certain things, such as beg for food, dig in the garden, or jump on the family couch.

So if a baby and a puppy get clear expectations, why wouldn't the professionals who work for you get the same advantage?

I recently spent the day with a sales manager in his office. This was an office with fairly low morale and extremely challenging circumstances. One of the reps who was assigned to answer the incoming phones wasn't at his desk at 9 a.m., and finally showed up at 10 a.m., an hour late.

Answering incoming phones represented about 40 percent of a sales rep's new business quota. When I asked Andrew, the manager, about it, he said, "I have that problem with this guy all the time—he shows up late at least once a week for his phone duty."

I asked Andrew what he had done to rectify the situation. Andrew: "I've asked him to make sure to come in on time, and he promises me he'll be here, but he still shows up late."

"There needs to be a consequence for these actions," I told Andrew. "You need to tell him that if he shows up late again, he'll lose his phone duty for a month."

"Now isn't the time to be delivering threats," said Andrew. As I mentioned, times were touch and morale was down in his office.

"You are right. The time to be delivering expectations was the day he started working for you. But now you have to do it—regardless of how bad the timing is."

If Andrew had clearly laid out his expectations when the rep started, and the consequences for failing to perform those actions, it would not have become a problem later on.

Setting expectations, and clearly communicating them, is mutually beneficial to both you and your team. In fact, there are three major areas of expectations you should deliver:

- ✓ What your team can expect of you
- ✓ What you expect of your team
- ✓ Where you want your team to be at the end of the:
    - ✓ Month
    - ✓ Quarter
    - ✓ Year

Whether or not you are in a sales management position, expectations are critical. And yes, this is going to require a lot of work and thought. But coming in prepared with these expectations can really help your team start in the direction you need them to go. In fact, the expectations you develop are really the blueprint for your goals and objectives. Your team cannot help you get where you want to go unless they are clear on where that place is!

But do not come in on your first day with your expectations. How can you know what needs to be done before you've even worked with your team?

Getting Started with Your New Team—Meeting with Your Boss

Before your first day, you should have a lengthy conversation with your new superior. Ask plenty of questions:

- ✓ What are the issues—positive and negative—with the team, as your superior views it?

- ✓ What are the goals your superior has for this team?

- ✓ What needs to be addressed immediately?

- ✓ What does your superior see in you that will help this team?

Why is this so important? There are several reasons:

- ✓ It helps you get your boss' support for what you are doing;

✓ It allows the boss to help set your framework for success; and

✓ You truly cannot get into trouble if things take a turn for the worse, because you can always tell the boss, "I am holding true to the values we discussed!"

The answers you receive from your boss will start laying the foundation for your expectations. But you need to do more than just talk to your boss.

Meeting with Your Team

During your first week, you should spend at least 15 to 20 minutes individually with each member of your team, from secretaries to senior salespeople. Ask probing questions. Get to know what they perceive as issues, along with any positives and negatives they perceive occur at the office.

In addition, you need to get to know them as individuals—where they live and what their life is about. I recently had a top sales rep talk to me about his manager. I ran into the rep, Brad, in a hallway at 7 in the evening at the office, and we ended up talking for 20 minutes, after I asked how he was doing. The conversation turned quickly to his boss, who worked for me.

"Andy is a really good guy, and I like him just fine," said Brad. "But his big failing is he doesn't know about any of us. I got married two weeks ago and he did not even mention anything to me. I honestly believe he couldn't tell you where I live, or whom I married, or anything about me that makes me an individual."

Andy, the manager, did talk with his team—but only

SETTING AND DELIVERING EXPECTATIONS

about things that interested Andy. Most employees want their boss to know about them: their life and their individual personal situations. No one is really interested in you. They want you to be interested in them.

If you asked me about the 250+ people who worked for me, I could probably come very closing to telling you where each lived, if they were married, and what their ultimate ambition was. It's important to them to have me know something about them and remember it.

My dad's strongest asset — and one I envy greatly — is that he never forgets a name. If you meet him once, he will remember your name. Casual acquaintances come up to me and remark on this all the time. What an attribute that is in a manager or executive! If you can walk into an office and call everyone by his or her name, or go to a company picnic and call spouses by their first name, the respect for you increases exponentially.

Now that you are aware of how critical it is to get to know your team as individuals, make sure to sit down with each of them, ask them about their situation and then turn it into business. Ask:

- ✓ "What do you want from a manager?"
- ✓ "What do you want changed and what do you want to stay the same?"
- ✓ "How can I, as a manager, help you succeed?"
- ✓ "What are your career ambitions and goals?"

It's really important to know what your employees want from their manager because you will need to adapt to what to their needs. I worked with a fellow sales rep that needed attention from her manager all the time. She worked in an office with me, about eighty miles from our boss. Tracy called him on the phone four or five times every day for lengthy conversations. The subjects were all over the place. She just wanted him to know what she was doing and how hard she was working.

At the same time, I talked to my boss only once a week — that was all I needed from him. Tracy was amazed that I talked with him so infrequently, but I knew the boss would be there for me when I needed him. I just preferred a lot of independence, and she wanted constant attention. As salespeople, we were both well over quota, but both of us needed entirely different management styles from our boss.

The second question — "What do you want changed?" — is a time to find out what you can do to help your employee and also what it is that frustrates them. You may not be able to implement all the changes he or she desires (and make sure never to over-promise on what you can and cannot deliver), but you are going to get a sense of what is on people's minds.

When I was in college, there was an annual musical and comedy show, and all of the fraternities, sororities and dorms each produced a twenty-minute skit. Part satire, and often a little raunchy, the skits could really skewer university life. The university president was always in attendance, even though he was often the butt of most of the jokes. When I asked him why he put up with that, he told me, "It's the one chance I get every year to really find out what is on the student's minds."

As a manager, the third question — "How can I help you succeed?" — is powerful if the employee is honest with you. As a manager, you are in a situation where you can greatly influence someone's career — to the positive or negative. Many people may need time to think about what you can do to help them. Give them that time. Get their follow up. You will be surprised at the answer, but make sure to continually update them on this issue

That last question can help you more in your job than perhaps any other. If you know what your people want to do, and if you help them achieve it, they will do just about anything for you.

Setting Expectations of Your Team

Now that you have input from your boss and your subordinates, it's time to figure out what your expectations are. Keeping in mind the core values you have, and the needs of the office, it's time to take pen to paper.

Setting the expectations of your team is critical because this is essentially what you hope to accomplish in your term as a manager. Among the issues that need to be addressed include:

✓ Production — Do you want it increased, and if so, by how much and how soon?

This is a dicey proposition. Unless corporate goals differ from your own, your boss almost certainly wants you to increase production over what it currently is. Yet you cannot set a random figure ("Each staff member is to increase production 20% over last year"). By talking with your team, you have discovered strengths and weaknesses in the office that should help you determine an appropriate number. Remember, you are setting expectations here and not saying how you are going to get there. We will do that later.

✓ Honesty and Integrity

I strongly believe these elements must be included in any formal or informal expectations of both you and your team. The sooner your team realizes you are committed to conducting your business and managing your team with the utmost honesty and integrity in all facets of business — the better. And there is no more opportune time to get that in front of your team than when you set your expectations of them. The statement can be as simple as, "Each team member will conduct their business with the utmost integrity and honesty."

What more can you ask of someone than this? And what easier thing can you ask of someone? At the core of this expectation is asking simply asking a team member to do the right thing. If they have a doubt, then they should ask you.

✓ Ask for — and expect - a high level of performance.

Of the hundreds of people who have worked for me, I would estimate that all except for one or two could improve the level of their performance. That doesn't mean working more hours or skipping lunch; it means improving what they do when they do it.

Actually, I do not believe the adage that many hours is the only path to success. On the contrary, I admire those who get the job done in as few hours as possible. It's not about hours worked; it's about efficiency during the hours you work.

I had an sales rep, Scott, who was an outstanding producer — consistently in the top 10 out of 600 company-wide. The hours he put in, however, were probably in the bottom 25 percent. Scott got to work at 8am and his wife liked him home no later than 5:15 p.m. But he got the absolute most out of those nine hours. He spent hardly any time socializing. Scott usually ate lunch at his desk, and he was incredibly efficient handling the mundane paperwork that would kill other salespeople.

Watching Scott led me to understand a major principle of sales management: It's not the hours you put in; it's your results that count.

Another thing I realized from Scott, although not related to this topic: He was not a prototypical "salesperson." Quiet, subdued, and conservative, he did not fit the mold of a plaid-jacketed used car salesman in days gone by. But because of his amazing discipline and focus, he became a highly successful person. The lesson I learned? It's not personality that sells; it's a focus on discipline.

✓ Ask for a commitment

Finally, make sure you ask your team for a commitment. It's not enough telling them what you want—you need to gain their assurance that they will commit to what you want.

Whenever I give a motivational speech, I always conclude with identifying what I want, then asking the audience if they will commit to what I asked for. "Stand up if you will commit to this goal!"

Most people will stand up. And there is no difference with your set of expectations. There is nothing wrong with asking them to commit to your expectations. If someone is unwilling to do this — you immediately know you have a problem.

Sit down with the individual and ask them why they are unable to commit. Again, you need to ask probing questions.

"Why can't you commit to this?"

"What are your concerns about this commitment?"

"What can I do to help allay your concerns?"

In my experience, the reluctant team members fall into two categories: Those who are afraid of committing, and those who know they cannot do it. In either case, you are going to have work to do.

The primary reason an employee is afraid of making a commitment to succeed is they actually are afraid! It may be that they're concerned you will make an issue out of it when it comes time for a performance appraisal or evaluation.

I had one employee who said, "But if I do not do it, you are going to hold it against me." I told her that it had nothing to do with holding it against someone. I believe that getting a commitment — whether or written or oral — provides a necessary impetus for getting people to step up and get you what you need.

If you get any other excuse, it's virtually certain that team member knows in their heart they cannot do it.

Now, no one is going to tell you, "I cannot do it."

The excuses will manifest themselves in many different ways. Again, you need to find out what their reasons are. And, if you are convinced they cannot do it, you are on the road to either helping that person succeed or helping that person find a new career opportunity.

Setting Expectations of Yourself

While the expectations you have of your team are *where* you want to go, the expectations you have of yourself determine *how* you are going to get there.

Each of us is blessed with unique gifts that allow us to help others. The key in this case is to know what you can and cannot do to help your team succeed.

A trite interview question is always, "Tell me about your strengths and weaknesses." While we'll get to that later, it is crucial that *you* clearly know what *your* strengths and weaknesses are.

I'll tell you a little secret that will help you succeed no matter what:

Always know what your strengths and weaknesses are. And always play to your strengths while minimizing your weaknesses.

My weaknesses are (as anyone who has worked directly for me can attest) disorganization and, for lack of a better expression, lack of attention to detail.

But those weaknesses are fine for two reasons: 1) I know what my weaknesses are; and 2) I find people to work with me who are strong in the areas of my weaknesses.

The best assistants I've ever had are totally organized

and have a command of detail. That way, they can remind me of things I have forgotten, which helps me focus on my strengths because I do not have to worry about my weaknesses. Come to think of it, I also appreciate most those team members who conduct the minutiae of their business independently, which allows me to focus on big picture stuff.

You are asking this of yourself: When setting expectations, maximize your strengths.

What can your team expect of you?

I always use this opportunity to emphasize the most important things I bring to the table—my ability to function for them as a rainmaker; allowing my team the freedom to work as independently as they can, running interference for them so they can be free to sell; and any other thing I can think of.

In addition to subtly mentioning your strengths, you should also identify the opportunities your team will have to communicate with you.

There is not a manager I know who doesn't boast, "I have an open-door policy." But what the heck does that mean?

To me, an open door doesn't begin and end with your office. An open door means you are available 24/7 to help them. (It doesn't hurt to remind your team to use your cell phone judiciously). But the days of the manager working in the office from 9 to 5 ended with the Reagan administration. Managers today must be available more than 9 to 5, since the demands upon us are clearly more than 9 to 5.

Tell your team when you are available. How they can contact you, and when it's appropriate to contact you.

I recently had a new manager who was hired without

a lot of experience. But his reputation was as a solid administrator with a great work ethic. Mark started in his district at a time when I was incredibly busy. I spent as much time with him as I could, but it wasn't enough. I gave Mark by cell phone and told him he should always call that number ANY time he had a question.

Sure enough, I would be at dinner, or in the shower, or in a meeting, and he would call. But I never told him I would call him back. To the contrary, I was thrilled that he would call me because that was emblematic of how much he wanted to succeed.

Another of the most important things your team wants is a manager who stands up for them. This can take the form of several guises, but most often it manifests with either a client who complains or internal bureaucracy that prohibits one of your employees from increasing productivity.

In either case, your team needs to believe that you are standing up for them. Your challenge is to accomplish that while ensuring your business objectives (customer service or needs of the organization) are met.

Most clients who complain about one of your team members believe that it was the employee who caused the problem. In my experience, this is hardly ever the case. Instead, it tends to be internal corporate issues, the client's fault, or miscommunication.

Whatever you do, always make sure to sit with your employee before you make any judgment on fault. Find out the employee's perspective on the complaint; it's virtually certain the employee will have a different version of the story than the client.

After you make your decision, and notify your client of the resolution, make sure to minimize the employee aspect of the problem. And if you determine it was the employee's fault, make sure to sit with him or her and offer a better way of handling the situation.

Another common problem is with an internal bureaucracy in a large corporation (read: politics) that makes you do things you or your team do not necessarily want to do.

My boss was on vacation once, and I got to spend two weeks in his shoes, frequently answering to the senior guy. It was a great learning experience for me until one day when the senior guy said, "I need more of your sales trainees to become full reps immediately."

Upon hearing this, my training manager had a fit. She wasn't ready to let trainees become full-fledged reps until they were thoroughly trained.

"Letting them out too early will be disastrous," she said. I was caught between a rock and a hard spot. I needed to stand up for my manager, while at the same time appease the needs of the senior guy.

The solution? I let the training manager call the senior guy directly and voice her concerns. Why let me be the conduit for her arguments and his? She appreciated the direct connection to the top, and the senior guy was surprised at the issues she raised which he never thought of. She got her way.

On the following pages are expectations I set of my team. There are three sets: one of my expectations of each team member; another was for my expectation of myself; and the last was what each person could expect of me. Every year I change the expectations, but every year they are always framed in my office.

Sample Expectations

Eric's Expectations of You
(Note: this was back in 1997
when I was managing sales reps.)

Each sales rep will:

- Be committed to achieving all goals in all lines

- Be committed to achieving team goals

- Have average annual sales rep income at $XX,XXX

- Believe in and perform two-way communication with management and attend all meetings on time

- Be committed to the concept of customer service as new business acquisition

- Take ownership of complaints and to refer as few complaints as possible to management

- Understand that it is not how many hours worked, but results that count

- Develop and adhere to a comprehensive business development plan to achieve mastery in all areas of business management

- Contact and report on all marketing leads within 48 hours

- Remember that the most important psychological part of the job is to have fun

- And ...live our theme: *"Work Hard, Play Hard!"*

Eric's Goals
(again from 1997)

I will:

- Earn $100,000 (that is $8,333 per month)
- Be recognized as the top district in the company
- Attend Sales Conference
- Have at least four salespeople qualify for conference
- Allow zero customer complaints from this office to reach the next management level

And…as always

1. Make a lot of money
2. Have fun!
3. To the extent possible, have peace and harmony in my job

What You Can Expect from Eric
(1997)

- A commitment is to give you as much information to help you do your job as possible

- An open door policy

- Formalized monthly one-on-one checkpoint meetings with each agent to review production and set goals for the upcoming month and quarter, and to discuss any issues and needs (but you are always welcome to talk at any time)

- A commitment to fostering an atmosphere of fun

- Risk-taking—as long as it is ethical—and to do whatever it takes to increase production and make everyone more money

- Frequent and positive recognition for tasks well done, for production, and for exceeding personal bests

- To be a "Rainmaker"—a consistent approach to helping you with production

- Zero tolerance for complaints, non-returned phone calls, and unanswered go-backs

- To remove as many obstacles as possible from you selling

- And every day, a commitment to "Work Hard, Play Hard!"

Let's have a great time!

Eric's Rules of the Road

Rules of the Road are a little bonus that takes setting expectations a step further.

Once upon a time, there was a billionaire by the name of Jerry Perenchio. Long before he became a billionaire, he was high school classmates of my uncle and friends with my mom. He wrote a treatise called "Rules of the Road," a guideline for how to work with him. It inspired me to write my own Rules of the Road as a way for my employees to better understand the expectations I have for them.

I currently have a number of HR professionals working for me, and I've been working with HR pros since 2001. There is a big difference with consulting (which is what we do) and being on staff. When you work as an HR pro for a company, you can say, "No, you cannot do that."

Not so, when you are a consultant.

So, after nearly twenty years of working with HR consultants and with a nod to Jerry Perenchio, here are Eric's Rules of the Road:

1. Take 100% responsibility for your actions.
2. Be relentless about your intellectual curiosity. Nothing makes you obsolete faster than refusing to learn new things.
3. It's all about results. I am not interested in *how*. I am interested in *if*.
4. Never say *no*. Your job isn't to tell someone they cannot do it, but how they can do it.
5. Sometimes the answer may actually be *no*, but do not

you think it is about being sure that you understand the outcome the client wants to reach?

6. Being late to a client meeting is unforgivable. Exception: calling the client and letting them know you are running late.

7. You are the Option King or Queen. If a client has a challenge, your role is to present options and the risks therein. Rarely is there just one way to solve a challenge.

8. Mistakes are never a problem. Mistakes are an opportunity to learn. Making the same mistake twice is a problem.

9. Never ignore an e-mail or voice mail, even if your response is, "Let me get back to you tomorrow." Clients do not like to be left hanging. (Neither do I!)

10. Have fun and project enthusiasm. No one wants to deal with a downer.

11. Minimize drama. We'll all live longer.

12. Care as much about your client as your client does. (You cannot care about a client's business more than your client cares about their business).

Setting Goals

You have set your expectations, and you have your core values. Now it's time to put your plan into action by establishing goals.

Goals have a purpose. They are specific, and they have a due date. That is what makes them different than expectations.

I am a huge believer in goals. I have never accomplished significant in my life without them. This is true both personally and in my professional life.

When I was thirteen, I set as a goal to become an Eagle Scout when I was seventeen. It happened.

When I was in my early twenties, I was having a lot of fun traveling inside the United States. I set a goal to set foot in all fifty states by the time I was thirty-five. It happened.

Obviously, I had to have professional goals. In 1987, I set out to be the top producing sales agent in my office. It happened.

In 1997, I set out to make my sales team the top producing office in my region. It happened.

But when my goals were ill-defined, vague or non-existent, it did not happen. In the early 1990s, I wanted to advance my career and make more money. I did so, but without a specific goal in mind. In 1995, I was floundering in a job I was ill suited for. Then, out of the blue, a regional sales manager asked me to lunch. He told me he thought I would make a great sales manager — a job I had never thought about. He offered me a job and two weeks later, I was managing a team of twenty people and was on my way.

It took me a short while to find my footing, and I did well in 1996. Then, I got back to specific goals.

In 1997, I set out to make my team the top producing office in my region. It happened.

In 2005, I decided I wanted to be president of a not-for-profit organization. Three years later, I was.

In 2019, I decided that I wanted to create a leadership program that took theory and research (what you learn at a business school) and bridge the gap between theory and practicality. In 2019, I launched that program.

So when my goals have been vague or not present at all, nothing has happened. When there were specific and with a deadline in mind, I have always succeeded. The same thing applies to you.

Raising the Bar

Whatever you are doing, and whatever it is you decide to do, the most important thing to do is raise the bar. This means doing better than has been done before. You are going to want to improve results over the previous regime.

Whether talking about production, efficiency, or customer satisfaction, it's critical to show improvement. At the end of the day, a manager is measured on results — and not how good a person he or she is. What does not matter is your sincerity, the time you put into your job nor the activities you conduct. What matters to the boss is results. You start creating better results by raising the bar.

And no manager has ever been able to raise the bar by *lowering* goals or expectations. A successful manager has to target an increase by raising goals and, as we've just seen, expectations.

So, the first step is to identify the areas in which you can improve and set the goal. Then, specifically state what you want to accomplish and the time by which you want it accomplished. This is a lot easier in sales than in a service business, but the idea is the same. You need to find a measurable area that is ripe for improvement, then set a goal and get it done.

Like your expectations, you want your goals written down, easily communicated and reasonable to attain. Likewise, the buy-in you get from your team is critical. Like a drill instructor conducting a review, you need to make sure they know what the goals are. They need to be able to repeat your goals verbatim and assume your goals as their own.

"It's our goal."

I once worked for a very enthusiastic manager who was almost as goal-oriented as I. Each time we had a meeting, we began by reciting the team goals, and even though this was many years ago, I can still recite them by memory:

> Be the #1 team in the company. The average agent will earn $X. And our customers will rate us a 9 on our customer service surveys.

It cannot get simpler than that. And boy, we really remembered those goals, because our manager checked it out every time he came by our desks. It may sound corny, or something you hear about in basic training for the armed forces, but it has a way of working.

The Power of Visualization

By now you realize that I am a believer in writing things down, especially expectations and goals. Always write down your goals, look at them daily, and review in your mind every step you need to get to where you are going. To be highly successful, you need to live and breathe your goals. In the morning you should be thinking of them. Before you go to bed at night you should be reciting them.

Have you ever sat at home with a lottery ticket when the jackpot is huge—say 60 or 70 million dollars? Did you fantasize about what you'd do if you won? The exact same concept applies here. It's the power of visualization.

I have seen many of my peers spend hours developing a comprehensive business plan, present it to the boss and get it approved, only to never revisit it again until it's time to update it next year. A good business plan is a road map for you and your team to get to your goals.

Your plan, and your goals, have to be revisited every day. Whether you look at them first thing in the morning, or right before you go home every night, you should always be visualizing your goals.

- "What am I doing today to accomplish my goals?"

- "What is my team doing today to get to our goals?"

- "What do I need to do to help my team get there?"

Your day should always be planned to answer those questions.

9

COMMUNICATION: THE KEY TO SUCCESS

"The only thing that TV and film directors have in common is the need to communicate with people. You need to communicate with your people in order to get your ideas across and to get your vision to the audience."

—William Friedkin, director of
The French Connection

There is no more important component to success in management than communication. In my experience, most managers fail because they cannot adequately communicate with their team.

Management begins and ends with communication. And while effective communication is the most important part of successful management, ineffective communication will sabotage you every time.

It is not so much WHAT you say, but HOW you say it that counts.

I had a manager working for me who was—to put it mildly—challenged when it came to people skills. A very smart guy, Andrew nonetheless had major trouble communicating with his team. One afternoon, he called me and said that one of his employees—Nora—might be calling me with a complaint about a "discussion" Andrew and Nora had recently.

Knowing something about Andrew, I asked him to describe what happened. It turns out that Nora was supposed to be answering the phones but left to take a bathroom break without finding a temporary replacement.

Andrew said, "I asked Nora what she was doing walking to the bathroom and not answering the phones. She said, 'I've got someone to replace me for a minute'. But there was no one there, so I told her to go back to her phone until she could find someone to replace her. Nora got mad and said she was going to call you."

Nora called me a few minutes later and she was indeed upset. When I asked her what happened, she quoted the conversation virtually word for word as Andrew had.

But she said, "Andrew was screaming at me. He turned red and for a minute thought he was going to hit me."

That was all I needed to here. I drove up to the office and discussed anger management with Andrew. When he realized what he had done, he immediately went to Nora and profusely apologized. He learned the most important lesson: it's not *what* you say but *how* you say it.

If Andrew had been calm and talked to Nora in a normal tone of voice, the incident would not have happened. Nora took offense to his tone, and not the content.

I spent some time with both of them, asking them to explain the rationale behind why they did what they did. Andrew was surprised that Nora thought he was going to hit her.

"I just raised my voice because I was a little irritated," he said. "I wasn't that upset."

After everyone had a chance to talk things through candidly, the situation diffused itself.

The art of communication is one area where I do feel comfortable from an academic standpoint. I took a number of communications courses in college, and I learned a great deal about interpersonal communications. Since then, I have continued to study communication. The most important thing I have learned (and witnessed) is that communication is not necessarily a natural talent. It can be learned. So even if you feel your communication skills are not the best, you can always improve them.

As a manager, you need to become a master of communication, both formally and informally in these three areas:

- ✓ One-on-one communication
- ✓ One-to-group communication
- ✓ Written communication

Communicating One-on-One

My advice for everyone who communicates with anyone is the same:

- Be as direct as you can
- Be as blunt as you can
- Do not mince words—directness only helps you in the end
- Know whom you are talking to.

In dealing with your team individually, you have got to first identify the needs of each individual. As you get to know your team, you will discover what each person requires in the way of communication.

When you meet with each person on your team, ask him or her what he or she expects of you. Then, make sure to follow up with informal conversation as often as you can.

I tell new managers they should be spending at least 60 percent of their time away from behind their desk. Sit with your team members while they work—not to put pressure on them, but to find out how they do what they do. The reason you were promoted to management was because you have something to offer. Make sure to provide suggestions on how they can improve.

While sitting with a team member, it's also a good time to ask questions about what they do and how they do it. People generally love talking about themselves or their job. This is a great way of bonding with your team. This intimacy becomes extremely important when it comes time to ask your team to do something for you. And make no mistakes: there will be a time when you need them to do it for you.

I had a boss, Earl, who absolutely despised communicating with his team. Earl was a brilliant man, but he did not want to spend any time talking to people. As a result, people were literally intimidated with him—a condition he did nothing to discourage. And when it came time to ask for a step-up in production, the team either could not or would not deliver for him.

A peer of Earl's, Susan, was exactly the opposite of Earl. She had teams in multiple locations and spent at least 80 percent of her time with the troops in the field. And her team loved her. She actually was her own best line supervisor. And at her team meetings, the fun and esprit d'corps was incredible. Her team ended up doing anything for her; they'd have taken a bullet for her. She knew everything about each individual—and not just personal items, but their strengths and weaknesses. She was able to call upon her on experience to help them with their weaknesses, and no one was better at touting their strengths, which she would shout to all who would hear.

A couple of minutes every day can be all it takes. People want to know — crave to know — that their boss cares about them. But you have to legitimately enjoy it; otherwise you will come across as contrived and phony.

One-to-Group Communication

Equally critical to communications success is your ability to effectively communicate in a group situation when you are in charge. Whether there are a few people in the room, or you are giving a presentation in front of 400 people, this type of communication terrifies even the most hardcore manager.

Yet a major component of successful communication is the ability to communicate in this format.

My best advice is to think before you speak. You may only get that one opportunity to properly tell your story.

I am a veteran of meetings. Oh, boy, am I ever a veteran of meetings. I spent days in a row where I never saw my office — meeting after meeting all day long. I've been in meetings with 100 people that lasted five minutes, and I sat in one memorable meeting with 20 other people where an actuary explained the way he determined insurance rates. It lasted nine hours.

The first step is to plan. Even for the smallest meeting, develop an agenda, and make sure to follow it. I also recommend giving all the participants a copy of the agenda so they feel part of the meeting as well.

Volumes have been written on conducting a successful meeting, so I'll limit this to a few areas that have been proven successful for me over the years.

Lessons I've Learned About Conducting Meetings

I've been very fortunate in my career to have the opportunity to spend hours conducting meetings and making presentations, three years in corporate training, speaking to groups of thirty or forty people, eight years in management conducting team meetings, and I speak professionally all over North America to audiences of thousands of people. Here are the lessons I've learned.

1. It's okay if you schedule an hour meeting that only lasts thirty minutes. Do not waste anyone's time if you do not have to. Never schedule a 30-minute meeting that will last an hour. Everyone will be upset and behind the rest of the day.

2. Schedule the meeting with plenty of advance notice. I worked for a person who would send us an e-mail on Friday afternoons for a Monday morning meeting. Since many of us were coming from far away and had busy schedules, it was difficult to accomplish and, quite frankly, rude. Another boss I had was the opposite—he'd send an e-mail asking everyone to give him four or five days that we'd be available for a meeting two months away. That is treating people with respect, although sometimes a little cumbersome.

3. Set expectations. I always expect my team to come to my meetings on time and with their calendar and

a pad to take notes. One of my all-time pet peeves is a team member who shows up late to a meeting. It wastes everyone's time. Once, I was co-chairing a meeting. At the appointed time, only four of twelve people were present. My co-chair nonetheless started the meeting on time and told the four, "I never punish the punctual." It's a point I always remember, and so should you.

4. Always start your meetings with some form of recognition. Even if you have to struggle to find a reason to recognize someone or something, do it.

5. Always conclude your meetings with an open forum. Encourage each person to express his or her views or concerns or opinions. You will be surprised how some people — who will never talk about concerns with you in an individual setting — will express their views in a meeting. And, if others agree, you will have stimulated an opportunity for improvement. Or, at the very least, your team will have vented some frustrations.

6. When you want to make an important point, always make sure to pause at the end of your statement and ask if everyone is clear.

7. When meeting with your team, schedule the team meeting on the same day and time each month. That way, your team can make their own arrangements in advance, knowing there will always be a meeting at 8 a.m. on the first Friday of every month, for example. I always scheduled my team meetings on the first

Friday of the month so I could review the previous month's production, acknowledge the top producers, and get everyone on the same page for the upcoming month.

Lessons I've Learned from Giving A Speech

Some day I'll write another book on this topic. I am not like a lot of people: I enjoy speaking in public and in front of large groups. I am also fortunate that I do not need to memorize a speech or read from notes to adequately communicate what I want to say. I usually just have a key word or two and go from there. So here is my "Top Ten" list of suggestions.

1. **You have to work at it to be successful**. I will share one of the most flattering comments I've ever received from anyone was after a presentation I made to 400 managers and executives at my company. A colleague walked up and said, "It's so easy for you. You are a natural."

   I want to tell you: there is nothing natural about standing up in front of 400 people, including every boss you've ever had, and speaking extempore for 20 minutes. It's about preparation.

2. **Slow down**. The most common problem with novice speakers is they get nervous, which in turn gets them to speak way too fast.

3. **Become a master of your topic**. You have been asked to speak because you know more than your audience does. Use that to your advantage. You are the expert

and your audience is not. (This is a variant of the old "imagining your audience in their underwear" gag, something I've never subscribed to).

4. **Say what you want to say in as few words as possible.** I've heard thousands of speeches from work and community leaders over the years, and the one thing the great speakers have is the ability to say what they want to say and get out. If you do not believe this, read the Gettysburg Address or Martin Luther King's "I Have a Dream" speech. Lincoln and King both gave two of the most memorable speeches in history and both lasted less than five minutes. Do not be verbose. You can be verbose when you write a book when people have the leisure and the ability to edit as they read. They do not have that luxury when they're sitting in the middle of an auditorium.

5. **Do not try to be funny.** There is nothing more irritating than a speaker who tells a lame joke or thinks they are an amateur comedian. Be pleasant, be direct, and be friendly, but don't try to be funny. If you really are funny (and most people aren't), it will happen naturally.

6. **Do not spend time telling people what you are going to say.** All the so-called experts tell you to spend the first few minutes outlining what you are going to talk about. Why? Do not tell people what you plan on saying later. Just tell them what you want to say now!

A Few Words About E-mail

Do not be misled into thinking e-mail is an appropriate communications tool. It isn't! Everyone is now using e-mail as a substitute for interpersonal communication, and it is greatly harming business and personal relationships. The development of team "communication" tools (Slack, Jabber, texting) hasn't made things any easier, so when I use "e-mail," I'm referring to all electronic messaging.

- ✓ E-mail does not replace the need for verbal communication
- ✓ E-mail should never be used when expressing any form of displeasure or dissatisfaction
- ✓ E-mail is — too often — substituted for one-on-one conversations and discussions.
- ✓ E-mail should primarily be used when disseminating information to a lot of people very quickly.

I am always amused by those people who tell me e-mail is an indispensable management tool. But just a few years ago, e-mail was not around at all. How did these geniuses get along without e-mail then?

The answer was, they communicated. Now, e-mail is taking the place of a conversation, or meeting, or discussion, and it's a tragedy.

A boss of mine managed a dozen managers and over twenty facilities. And he would spend six hours every day on his e-mail. Everything: bad news, good news, FYI's would pop up on e-mail. I would leave work on

Thursday, go on a three-day vacation, and come back to the office on Monday at 6 a.m. to find over 100 e-mails — all from the boss. And this was in 2001! (He's retired now, and I shudder to think what it would look like today.)

What is especially funny about this is that when e-mail first became mainstream, this boss had to hand-write his messages and have his secretary send the e-mail because he did not know how to use the system! Once he learned it, however, it was brutal on all of us.

Unfortunately, he used e-mail as a substitute for visiting his team in remote locations, so he was never able to visit personally with his troops — they only knew of him by e-mail. Once, I asked him how he got along prior to the advent of e-mail. He couldn't come up with an answer.

One of my boss' peers, Dan, a manager I admired greatly, took the opposite approach, which was that e-mail is a necessary evil. He spent virtually all of his time in the field with his troops, returning to the office at night to review his e-mail and return phone calls. He had a policy of not leaving for home until all his messages from e-mail and voice mail were returned.

Dan never sent a group e-mail when things were bad, or when he was displeased. Instead, he got his management team on a conference call. His communication style was much more personal, and he got much more done than my poor boss who spent six hours a day on e-mail.

E-mail should be a time saver and not a time waster.

There is nothing wrong with sending a note to congratulate a top performer or to motivate someone who needs cheering up, but poor managers believe it is a form of interpersonal communication. In fact, the best compliment stills comes in the form of a hand-written note from the boss, followed up by a personal visit or at least a phone call. As we continue to grow in an electronic age, employees will more and more value the personal touch.

Here is another story that you might be able to relate to: In 2006, I was working with a digital marketing firm on improving their time management skills. I spent a couple of days at their office trying to determine what exactly was taking up so much time. I was sitting with a young lady and she seemed to be spending a lot of time texting.

I finally asked, "Who are you texting?"

"Devon."

I was flabbergasted. "You mean Devon, who's sitting fifteen feet over there?"

"Yes. I am frustrating because he's not responding to my texts."

I walked over to Devon, brought him to the young lady I was working with, and made them talk. It took three minutes.

I've been part of the workforce pre e-mail, which was about 1997, and post e-mail. I remember distinctly the joy I had went I received an e-mail. (AOL's famous "You've Got Mail!" was a sign someone cared about you.)

Yet, in less than a generation, e-mail has gone from exciting and thrilling to the bane of our existence. The average U.S. worker now spends 25 percent of their day reading or answering e-mails. The averaging mobile phone user checks their device 150 times every day. And largely as a result of these "time savers," 40 percent of the U.S. population believe it is impossible to succeed at work and have a balanced family life.

Employees now feel obliged to check their e-mails while on vacation. Now, having an untethered vacation is a dream many feel is elusive. (I can assure you, prior to about 2000, every vacation I had was untethered. How did we ever survive?)

As a manager and leader of people, the best advice I can give you is to be clear that you do not expect 24/7 slavish devotion from your employees to their job. Evenings and weekends are work-free time. If you empower this advice, you will find employees who are more appreciative of you, their work, and less likely to burnout and leave. I love hiring people who worked in the entertainment industry because they appreciate that I do not expect employees to be available to me 24/7. It shows respect and that you care about them as people, not just as employees.

10

INSPECTING WHAT YOU EXPECT

We've spent the first four chapters of this book talking about core values, expectations, goals, and how to communicate.

None of these skills will do you a bit of good unless you are able to ensure what you've asked is being done. You have to inspect what you expect.

If you ask for something, you have got to make sure it gets done. If you do not follow up, people will assume it was unimportant. And trust me, the more you do this, the easier it gets.

I worked for an executive named Bill. Bill was very well liked and respected by all of his team for his work ethic and great people skills. But as Bill got busier and busier, he developed the habit of taking all of his paperwork and memos home on Friday nights and reading them during the weekend. And we got used to having a pile of stuff on our desks every Monday morning with, "See me on this!" or "Please perform an evaluation on this and get it to me by lunchtime on Monday."

There were twenty of us in the department, each with five to ten "to do's" from Bill. As you can imagine, that meant every Monday was like a ten-hour-long fire drill, with people running around, trying to get information and writing reports to get done by Bill's deadline.

Then something funny happened. Someone said, "I went to see Bill this morning and he couldn't remember why he wrote, 'see Me' on this paper."

Well, that gave the rest of us the idea that if Bill couldn't remember all of the things he wrote us over the weekend, he couldn't possibly need everything he asked about for Monday morning.

One Monday, we all tried an experiment. None of us turned in any report by Monday at lunch. And nothing happened! A couple of days later, Bill asked a couple of people if they had finished a certain report yet. They quickly determined that specific report was the real priority for the boss, and they promptly turned it in.

The lesson we learned was: unless Bill asked for it again, it must not have been that important to begin with. And we ignored all of those Monday morning "to-do's" and got on with our jobs. Bill's lesson was: if you ask for it and expect it, you need to inspect it.

Remember Where You Came From

This lesson becomes increasingly important as you move up the chain of command. I remember when I was first promoted, in 1990, from sales agent to sales trainer. My fellow agents and I used to always joke about the management and executives at our company, and the worst thing we could think of was they "forgot where they came from", meaning that did not understand our jobs the way they used to when they had our jobs.

So, when I got the promotion, all my friends said, "You better not forget where you came from." Of course, that is easier said than done. Because as you become more and more removed from the line job, the easier it is to forget what that job was really like on a day-to-day basis.

Look, you cannot help but forget where you came from when you are doing another job. But you can recognize this problem and do everything you can to control it.

The best way to remember where you came from is to spend time with the people who do what you used to do—inspecting what you expect at all times and observing what your team members do.

An important side benefit of this is you will get renewed respect from your team when they realize you really do understand what they do.

I've seen many executives rise to the top of the ivory tower, only to become so immersed in the activities in that ivory tower they lost empathy and compassion for the problems of the rank-and-file. When I saw this, I vowed—and so should you—never to forget where I came from.

11

INSTILLING PASSION

I am not a great fan of the word *motivation*. First of all, it implies something you do to someone else that they may not want in the first place. Secondly, I believe you cannot motivate someone; they can only motivate themselves.

Think about it: How often have you ever been able to force someone to do something they do not want to do? I do not have children, but I've observed my friends try to do this with their children. Even though the parents have the authority, getting the kid to do something the kid doesn't want is pretty brutal. The parents resort to bribery or begging or some equally demeaning activity.

It's the same with adults. People are all motivated to do *something*; your job is to discover what it is that motivates them.

So my preferred term is *passion*. I believe it is the job of every manager to instill passion in their team—a passion for doing their job, for living their life, etc.

The interviewer Larry King was once asked who his favorite person to interview was. I'll never forget his answer: "Anyone who has passion, regardless of who they are or what they do. If they have a passion for what they do, they are a great interview."

Passion Defined

The first reaction from most people when they hear the word *passion* is to think of it in the romantic sense. But I am using it here in the sense of enthusiasm, zeal, excitement and delight.

Here is a question to ask yourself. I ask it of myself all the time and frequently ask it of my team:

Why would you spend your life doing something you do not truly enjoy?

You spend at least a third of your life at work. Maybe more. Obviously, you get paid for what you do, but there are a lot of jobs out there and a lot of companies that would happily employ you. So why do you do what you do and where you do it?

I sincerely hope it's because you enjoy what you do, because if it isn't, you should look for another job. Life is too short to not enjoy.

I firmly believe you must be passionate about what you do. You must look forward to going to work and making decisions and helping people and achieving goals and succeeding. This cannot be made up; you have to be genuine about it. I spent a long time trying and hoping, planning to get where I got. When I got there, I was going to make the most of it.

It Comes from Within

First, last and always, passion comes from you. You cannot possibly expect anyone else to have the passion unless you've genuinely got it yourself. You set the tone for your team. Your mood and attitude will always dictate the atmosphere in the office.

Susan, a manager I respected greatly, called it "always being on stage." Whether you know it or not, whether you *believe* it or not, people are always watching you and judging you when you are a manager. You set the tone with every statement you utter and every gesture you make.

It's all about attitude. Your team responds to your emotions and your beliefs, whether you think you are hiding them or not.

When I was in sales training, I prided myself on being entertaining. (I wasn't a very good trainer, but I tried to be fun.) I was training a class over the course of a couple of weeks, and I was enjoying the class and it was pretty obvious they were responding to me as well. Then one day, I went into work in a foul mood (fortunately my memory has blanked it completely out as to why this was). I took a deep breath before walking into the class and promised to keep my problems out of the class.

I thought I did well. The class laughed at my jokes and was reasonably involved. No one ever said anything to me.

But when the class ended, I reviewed the instructor evaluations. I got good marks, except that several students wrote, "Eric is the best trainer — when he's in a good mood." That really stung, and all that time I had no idea that anyone knew I was in a bad mood.

It was a great lesson. You have to be genuine and you are not allowed to be down. It's all about attitude, and a smile from you will always improve the passion of your team. Always be positive, and try never to show any weakness. Your team looks to you to be a leader, and you must demonstrate to them every day that you act like a leader.

Of course, there are going to be days where you are down. You don't have to fake happiness, but be genuine. If you are not in the mood to be entertaining, state as much, and do you best to be helpful.

The Mirror

You have to determine the best way to instill passion in your team, but I'll share with you some of the words and themes I use when talking about passion with my team, and those of others. You can use these by yourself, in determining the level of passion you have, or with your team to attempt to increase their level of passion. You have probably seen flecks of this and that, spread throughout this book, but it's consolidated here.

I call this technique the mirror, because passion, pride and motivation cannot possibly come from anyone else than the person in the mirror. I live in America, and in America no one can force you to do anything — especially the desire to do one's job better.

Therefore, it is only up to you to succeed. You must enjoy what you do. As I ask you the following questions, be as brutally honest as you can with yourself when answering them.

✓ Are you having fun in your job?

✓ Do you take pride in the job you are doing?

✓ Are you eager to go to work every day?

✓ Do you want to win?

✓ Do you have the drive to succeed?

If you cannot answer *yes* to each of these questions, find another job. Life is too short to spend your time here doing something you do not love. And make sure to tell that to your team members you are not meeting your expectations!

The Drive

In the final analysis, it's not about obstacles; successful managers find ways of overcoming any obstacles (or, at least, minimizing the most difficult ones). It isn't about a fancy office, or corporate changes or anything else. It is about the drive. And the drive only comes from within.

Here are the characteristics of people who have the drive:

Endurance
Excellence, passion, drive and spirit are easily given and manufactured over a short period of time. Yet the truly outstanding people demonstrate this consistently, over a long period of time. I always admired the salespeople who, year in and year out, excelled. Anyone can put together a good month or good quarter, or good year — but it's the ones who do it over a long period of time who get my respect.

Passion

As I've said, if you do not have passion for what you do, you shouldn't do it. I've known more people — good people — who simply did not have their heart in their job, and they could not find a way to succeed. Do not waste your life doing something you do not truly want to do.

Perseverance

Most businesses I've observed are cyclical. And unquestionably there will be tough times as well as good. Successful people find a way to maneuver through the ups and downs that are inevitable in business. The long-term view — rather than immediate gratification — allows these people to succeed.

Patience

One of my worst characteristics is impatience. I've seen it on my performance reviews, heard it in comments from my teams and bosses, and even my parents have given me grief over it. I need to be more patient than I am. So do a lot of people I know. Patience, to some degree, equates to maturity. Maturity indicates the wisdom to know that the vagaries of everyday work should not dictate your mood, change your optimism, nor ruin your day. Patience means you rise above the little things in life to become the best.

On the other hand, there are times where patience must naturally run thin. Some examples:

✓ Long-term performance continues to stagnate or decline,

✓ A chronic under-performing employee, and

✓ A team that is underperforming or consistently unhappy.

In these cases, good managers create a sense of urgency.

Creating a Sense of Urgency

How many times have you either had this conversation with an employee, or had it with a superior?

"We have to do better."

"How?"

"I do not know, but our production is down and management is on my case to improve things right away."

Sound familiar? This conversation, or variants of it, takes place in business every day.

A myriad of problems exist with the above statements (we'll talk about taking ownership in the next chapter), but the one to focus on here is the failure by the manager to create a sense of urgency. It must be done. Set deadlines and follow through to make sure those deadlines are met. Deadlines create an instant sense of urgency. For example, I start client projects by asking the client when the due date is for a report. I then work backwards. I do my best work when up against a deadline. Without that deadline, I would never get anything done.

Adversity Doesn't Breed Contempt

Adversity, if managed properly, can breed more success than a manager ever dreamed of. Great leaders do not avoid or fear trouble; they embrace it. President Clinton often remarked his legacy would be incomplete without a major world conflict or trouble.

In sports, championship teams often become more closely bound during a losing streak, or lonely times on the road. Many great coaches know this and use it to their advantage.

I am not a mathematician, but Here is a formula that I advocate and believe in:

$$Adversity + Discipline = Success$$

The path to greatness almost always must go through some adversity. Once a team — whether it be your team or the Los Angeles Lakers — hits a snag in the road, it's up to the leader to direct them out and towards success.

But, with proper management and a strong sense of discipline, adversity is the first step towards your success.

What adversity does you and your team face? Identify what that is, and make sure everyone on your team is aware of it. Make sure to get their agreement that whatever the problem is, it is indeed serious. These problems could be:

- ✓ A new corporate policy that will result in lowered production,
- ✓ An increase in workload without additional staff to perform it, or
- ✓ Inheriting a team that has never excelled.

Now, it's time to make a plan that takes you from trouble to triumph.

Strategically Instill a Fear of Loss

What are the ramifications for your team members if what you think will happen, happens? Lowered commissions; more working hours; more stress; less opportunity for advancement?

Let's take a look at the three problems listed above and instill a fear of loss as a result of them.

- *A new corporate policy that will result in lowered production*

This is near and dear to my heart, because I've had to manage this situation many times in my career. Here are a couple of options:

1. Determine how much money your team members could lose because of the new policy (there is the loss). Spend a weekend with a yellow legal pad, writing down every way you can think of to increase income through other means. Talk to your peers—get their ideas as well. Then discuss with the group ways you can mitigate the damage of the policy.

2. Set the table with a doomsday scenario. If your team does not adapt these new ideas, what will the concrete results be? What does a 20 percent production loss mean in terms of lost commissions, or wages? Sit with each person who works for you and do the math. Can they afford to maintain the status quo, or do they need to change?

One of my managers, Jason, had poor production in a product line that did not generate much income, but it was part of his job and those of his team to achieve quota in all business lines. I was constantly grinding on Jason, asking what he was doing to increase the production in this product line. Finally, I couldn't stand it any longer, and went to his office to meet with him and each of his reps individually.

Prior to meeting with a veteran rep, Jason and I reviewed his production over the past year. George was a long-term rep but only an average producer. And in the product line I was concerned about, George was ghastly. Jason went on to say that even though was an average producer, making decent money, he married a woman who made a substantial amount of money. In addition, George inherited a beautiful home near the beach. So, George was not greatly concerned about money, and he generally came into work around 10 and left around 4.

When George walked into the conference room, we asked him about his production in the specific product line. George said that it was just too hard to write and not worth the trouble it took to write. What Jason did next made me proud.

Jason: "You understand that it's part of your job requirement to write this line?"

George: "Yes, but it's just not worth it and too difficult."

Jason: "Okay, Here is the deal. I want to find out how hard it is. You do a decent job for me in everything else, but I've been talking to you about this for months. I am not kidding around—if you do not have four widgets in this product line by the end of this month, then you are going to spend two nights a week with me soliciting this business until your production improves. I'll work right with you, getting you leads and helping you contact and sell prospects. In fact, I'd be happy to work with you. But I suspect you'd rather get it on your own."

George (after a very long silence): "I'll see what I can do."

George ended up with six widgets that month and continued on after that. I asked Jason why he did what he did.

Jason said, "He values his lifestyle a great deal, getting home early and spending time with his family. I knew the reason he wasn't writing the product was because he's lazy. I gave him an alternative that would alter his life, and I knew he did not want to change his life."

Jason strategically instilled a fear of loss with George. He was polite, professional, and direct with George. And both of them got what they wanted: Jason got his production and George maintained his lifestyle.

- *An increase in workload without additional staff to perform it*

One of my managers lost two of his four support staff in an office that could barely manage even with all four people. Obviously, his first priority was to hire two additional people, but the process took a few weeks, then — once hired — those people needed to be trained for another month.

During the two months he was short staffed, Mike was scrambling to serve the threefold needs: client service, support of his team, and support to and of the two remaining staff members.

Everyone on Mike's team — his salespeople and existing support staff — was deeply concerned about how the office could function. Anticipating the problem in advance, Mike and I developed a plan of action during those two months.

First, we held a meeting with the team. Mike outlined the problem. I told the team I was there and involved because I believed it to be a serious problem and one that would require everyone's support. We painted a picture of what would happen if the team did not change their focus during the next couple of months. Lowered production, decline in service quality, and additional pressure on the existing support team were just three of the areas which we mentioned.

During the meeting, we outlined our plan of attack, which included several areas, including getting support staff from nearby offices on the busiest days and deferring many incoming phone calls to those offices as well.

But we needed buy-in from the team in several areas. Since the office got extremely busy during the traditional lunch hour, we asked the two remaining service reps to delay their lunch until after 2 p.m. We asked the outside salespeople to help cover the service work when times got exceptionally busy. We assured them we would get the replacement team members hired and trained as quickly as possible.

We made sure to consistently praise everyone who helped out. Mike spent a lot of hours answering phone calls and doing service work. He was also in constant communication with the support staff—making sure they were okay, not overworked or under-appreciated. We even threw a barbecue lunch for the team at the end of the first month as a thank you for their effort.

What happened during those two months was a classic example of adversity breeding success. Everyone pitched in and helped out. The team became closer. Production did not suffer, and service quality remained the same.

The critical component to success was getting the buy-in of the team. Once assured that top management was aware of the problem and sincerely working to solve it, the team knew that it was ultimately up to them to succeed.

- *Inheriting a team that has never excelled*

I know a lot about this from two perspectives — one where I made it work, and one where I did not.

Let's start with when I did not. I changed companies and inherited at the same time a team that hadn't excelled in several years. There were various reasons and excuses for it, but it just hadn't happened. From the existing team, I heard every possible reason: poor marketplace, bad product, lack of support, etc. After accepting the position, I realized how serious the position is and remembered a serious tenet of management — you are only as good as the people you work with. After meeting individually with the team, I met with my boss and advised him that the situation was bad — and would probably get worse before it got better. Needless to say, that is not what he wanted to hear!

I divided the team into two categories:

- People who were trying but not succeeding; and

- People who were not trying.

With those who were not trying, I simply got rid of. If someone does not want it, there is literally nothing a manager can do—you cannot do the job for someone else. I focused my attention on those who were trying and helped them do better. Where I went wrong was in the hiring of replacements. Those people ultimately did not want to succeed as much as I did.

When your team does not succeed, it may not be your fault, but it is your responsibility.

When you do get the turnaround, the opposite affect occurs; however, make sure not to take the credit and spread it around your team. People know that the team is succeeding—they admire it when their leader points credit at the team. Joe Torre, the MLB's chief baseball officer and former manager of the New York Yankees, was particularly adept at this. When the team was playing well, he gave all the credit to the players. When the team was playing poorly, he shouldered the blame.

I worked once for a manager who was renowned for getting his people promoted. Hubert was very tough to work for—highly demanding and a workaholic. He lived two hours away from the office, but he'd be in the office every morning at 6 a.m. and left after 7 p.m. For those of us who shared in his drive—we loved working for him because he never took credit for anything—he gave us all the credit. He once called me into his office with a training idea and asked me to develop it. A couple of weeks later, he surprised me by bringing me into a group of top corporate executives and explained to them that this program was terrific, it was my idea, and I was the one who developed it. Soon after that, I received a major promotion.

I wasn't the only employee that happened to. By not taking credit, Hubert made sure that his people got promoted. The benefits to Hubert were twofold: with a reputation like that, everyone in the company wanted to work for him, and throughout the company, there were dozens of people in management who were extremely loyal to Hubert. By not taking credit, Hubert built himself a very long and very successful career.

12

TAKING OWNERSHIP

My major message here is: *Treat your operation as if it were your own.*

Success means treating your business as if it were your own. That is true for everyone—from the greatest entrepreneur to a PBX operator.

Imagine for a moment that it's your business that you are running, that you had the final decision-making power for every decision and could not be questioned, second-guessed or overruled. What would you do differently? What cost controls would you put into place? What incentives would you provide for your workers? What attitudinal changes would you implement? Who would you hire or fire?

You must treat your team as if you owned the business and were not merely an employee. Every decision you make needs to come from this perspective. Oh, I can hear your objections already. Let me try to refute them.

- *Well, it's nice to think I own the company, but since I have to report to someone, I cannot make unilateral decisions on my own.*

Possibly you cannot make every decision on your own without direction from above. But I've never met a competent manager who did not encourage the team to be proactive — to voluntarily make suggestions. After all, my managers see their day-to-day operation at ground level. And as much as I'd like to think I am totally a hands-on manager, my line managers knew more about their business than I ever did. So I welcome their decisions and suggestions, and unless it's cost-prohibitive, I'll always approve their suggestion.

My senior boss, Frank, had a great reputation as a sales-oriented executive. And any time we came to him with a suggestion, he never said *no*. What a wonderful attitude in an executive! He would let us make the decisions (of course, we ended up living or dying by those decisions, but that is only fair).

Frank's weakness was that he wasn't exactly a long-range thinker. I asked him about it once, and he said he wasn't even a good short-range planner. For several years, Frank held an annual three-day meeting in Palm Springs. That was the upside. The downside? It was always held in the middle of August, when the average temperature was about 110 degrees. And, unfortunately, he never got around to planning the agenda until the week before the meeting. As a result, for three years in a row, Frank would ask me and my three peers to put together a one- or two-hour presentation for all of the management team, on a subject he chose, such as "Adding Value" or "Advanced Sales Management." And we were given about three days to do it. That meant sixteen-hour days putting together a strategy, getting it on paper, getting executive approval, and then putting together a PowerPoint presentation. Needless to say, it was three hectic days.

When the annual meeting was approaching for August, I sent Frank an e-mail in early June, asking him if it would be okay if the four of us met and recommended a topic for our August presentation. Not only did he say *yes*, but he also asked me why it took so long to be proactive! It was a valuable lesson: the best managers *encourage* proactivity.

I worked closely for a few years with an operations manager at my company. His job was to literally manage about 60 people and a large operation for about 7,000 clients. Located in a marketplace a long way from most places, he was the ultimate example of running his operation like his own. In fact, the branch was called "Jack's Branch" and not the location name because he ran it his way and not the corporate way.

I once teased him about that, and instead of joking in kind, he responded seriously: "If the company is telling me to run the business as if it's my own, then that is what I am going to do. I know the clients and this market better than the people at our regional office or corporate headquarters, and I am going to do it the way I see best."

It may come as no surprise that Jack's Branch was one of the best run in the nation. He won awards for having the lowest employee turnover year after year and the highest client retention as well.

Jack's other advice, in the same conversation, was about "owning versus renting," a concept advocated by management gurus over the years. You either own your business, or you are renting, and anyone who rents is not going to treat their business or property the same way as someone who owns it. Jack was entrenched in this area — great home, good schools, and he had no intention or desire of ever getting a promotion that would remove him from his life.

He believed that contributed to his success: "If you know you are only going to be in a position—any position—for a short while, you are going to make decisions impacting your success for the short term. You will not be as successful in that position as you will be if you know you are in it for the long haul. When I make decisions, I am thinking how it will impact me for the long term. If you know you are going to be gone soon, there is no way you are going to make those same decisions."

- *I wish I had the authority to hire and fire people, but I have to get approval from Human Resources and Legal to do this. It isn't easy.*

Most managers do not have autonomous authority to hire (or, in some cases, fire). So what can you do in this area to treat the business as your own?

By communicating, observing and reviewing results with your team, you have a good sense of who is qualified for promotion and who isn't cutting the mustard. That—in itself—is a great start.

Once you have identified the people who have an opportunity for advancement, use that to your advantage. Spend additional time with them. Be direct—tell them that you have an eye on them for the future. Ask them if advancement is what they want. And then provide them with additional challenges and projects that can test their mettle. When they interview for a new job, they can truthfully say they've handled advanced tasks. Make sure to praise them to your superiors as often as appropriate. As we've seen from Hubert, getting a reputation as a manager who gets his people promoted is a great reputation to have.

At the same time, there are going to be team members who are not getting the job done. Without disciplinary action, or termination, you can also help those people on their way. Be direct—tell them they are not getting the job done, and offer concrete examples of why. Ask them if they are happy in their job, or if they'd be happy elsewhere. Create a sense of urgency by telling them the truth—if you do not see improvement, the writing will be on the wall. Most employees who are not doing well know it, and once they hear that statement from a manager, they will find opportunities elsewhere.

You will be surprised how well most people react to this conversation if you handle it properly. It cannot be a one-way conversation—it's critical you get as much input from the person as possible.

You should repeat one question over and over: "What can I do to help you with what you want?"

If the team member wants to find opportunities elsewhere, you should do some career counseling—offer suggestions for other jobs, based on your assessment of their strengths and weaknesses. If you have contacts with other companies, offer to call those people. This technique is called, "counseling out." It's an effective way to get rid of someone without the hassle and potential liability of firing someone.

If the team member is happy in their job, then he or she needs to clearly understand your expectations if they are to stay in that job. Every time that person does something inappropriate, or does not meet your expectations, you immediately need to correct that behavior.

Do not finish the meeting until you are completely satisfied that both you and your team member are on the same page. Reiterate what was said and both of your

action plans. Conclude by setting a time—perhaps a
week from now—when you will get together to review
progress.

- *It's not my decision!*

There is no easier way of losing the respect of your
team than to not take responsibility for a decision.

There are very few people in corporate America who
can make unilateral decisions. All of us—even senior
management—have to take orders now and again. And
some of those orders are not going to be one's that you
like!

You've got three choices:

✓ Say that you do not agree with the decision;

✓ Say it was a bad corporate call; or

✓ Say "let's work together and find a way of making
this work."

I hope you realize that the third option is clearly the
way to go. If your team discovers that you are merely an
order-taker, a conduit between superiors and associates,
then you will immediately lose their respect.

Team members want their manager to be a decision
maker and to take responsibility for those decisions. No
one wants to believe their boss is merely a pawn for the
executive staff. "It's not my decision," indicates you do
not have authority. And communicating that you do not
have authority is the worst decision you can make.

13

THE BIG LIE

I cannot tell you how many times I've sat in a Human Resources meeting, or a management seminar, and heard the speaker say something to effect of:

> "Always make sure to treat all of your employees exactly the same."

Nonsense! This is one of the biggest fallacies in management today.

People *do not* want to be treated the same; they want to feel special.

I have seen lots of places where workers are treated the same: They're found in aging factories on assembly lines, in Third World Countries, and in sweat shops. And all of those businesses are failing because they could not adapt to the changing needs and demands of today's worker.

All people want and need different things from their manager: some want to be left alone, some want constant reassurance, some want public recognition, and others need only private praise.

I distinctly remember the day I learned this lesson. I was a new manager, supervising a team of twelve outside salespeople and five inside reps. At my second team meeting, I singled out several people for outstanding performances during the previous month. I was particularly effusive in praise for Adele, an excellent rep who won virtually every corporate contest and was one of the top reps in the company. I vaguely noticed at the time that Adele wouldn't look me in the eye when I was talking about her, but did not pay much attention to it.

Later that day, I really noticed Adele was very quiet, so I walked over to her office and asked her if everything was okay. She said that it was not, and asked to see me in my office.

When we settled in, she told me, "You really embarrassed me by talking that way in front of the whole team. It made me totally uncomfortable."

I was completely surprised and told her so. "You are one of the top reps in the company, and you had a fabulous month. I thought you would appreciate the fact that I was singling you out for praise. And when I was a rep, I loved having that type of attention."

"No, that embarrasses me. And I think it makes my peers jealous of me. When you are happy with what I do, I want you to notice it, but just tell me in private — not in front of everyone else."

I learned my lesson fast and never again made a fuss about Adele in front of the team. But the true lesson was that people are not the same, and therefore want to be treated differently.

Another of my reps at the time, Rob, was a rebel. He was a true rocker, complete with long hair, a goatee, and earring. In a company that was very conservative, he went against the grain with dark purple dress shirts and fancy shoes. He was an exceptionally talented salesperson, but had been struggling during the past couple of years.

When I took over the district, my boss told me about Rob and said, "You need to make him more corporate. I want to see his hair cut and wear white dress shirts."

I was dreading that conversation with Rob. So I turned the tables a bit on him.

During our first one-on-one meeting, I told Rob that I was under some pressure to get him to become more corporate. But, I said, "I do not care a whit about that, and neither will my boss if you are hitting the right numbers. If you can get your production up, I will make sure that you can keep your hair at any length you want. But if you cannot do the job, I am not going to have a choice."

And that was the beginning of a great business relationship. He appreciated my candor, and I appreciated his production. That year, he finished in the top 10 percent of the company.

Did I treat Rob differently than my other people? Absolutely. Did I get from him what I needed? Absolutely.

The key to remember is that you need to ask everyone on your team what he or she wants from you. Then, you have to deliver.

So make sure to treat people differently—they need it.

Now that I've ranted about treating people differently, there is a kernel of truth about all those Human Resource-types who talk about treating people the same.

Swenson's Rule of Managing People Successfully is:

You can treat people differently, but make sure to treat them consistently.

When you properly treat people differently, you leave yourself open to accusations of favoritism. No one wants a manager who plays favorites. It creates a very poor environment in the workplace.

You can easily dismiss charges of favoritism the way I did — by telling your team in a meeting:

"Yes. I play favorites. If you are making your numbers, you can do whatever you want as long as it is legal and ethical. If you are not making your numbers, you are going to be treated differently."

I first learned this lesson in 1986, working for my first manager. Allan, at that time, was 67 years old, a product of the mines in Ohio and West Virginia. And after 35 years in management with the company, Allan was accustomed to getting his own way — he terrorized everyone: employees, his superiors, customers, everyone. He was a legend in the company, and no one wanted to work for him. (Naturally, as a tenderfoot right out of college, I did not have the luxury of knowing this in advance). We would have meetings where he would have half the team in tears. When he got on a roll, people had to look out. Screaming, yelling, hand waving: all of these were elements of a standard Allan meeting.

He could never make it as a manager in today's environment, where the slightest misspoken word can lead to a lawsuit or where many employees go running to Human Resources or their attorney without much justification.

But the one thing Allan did was to treat everyone the same. If we did our job, he left us alone. If we did not, there was no end to the grief he caused us. And although no one in the company wanted to work for Allan, everyone who worked for him (and was successful) totally respected him. Out of fourteen reps in that office, five ended up in management, and all of us learned a lot of valuable lessons.

14

Mistakes and Responsibility

I tell all my employees about my philosophy of mistakes, which goes like this:

There are a lot of people who have never made a mistake. Almost always, they are the people who have never risked anything in their lives. Always give me people who are willing to make a decision on their own, as opposed to people so scared of making a decision they wait until the boss is around.

I want risk-takers working for me. As long as they do not make the same mistake twice, they are welcome to make decisions with the possibility of error.

A valued colleague of mine says, "I would rather finish first, while being 80% right, than finish second while being 100% right."

At the end of the day, it's where you finish, not how you got there.

Be a Decision Maker and Take Responsibility

Mark, a new manager whom I inherited, had been a 25-year assistant manager before finally being promoted to his first management position. He also went from essentially a bureaucratic position into a sales management position, which demanded a lot more creativity and instant decision-making than he had been used to. I spent hours with him, reviewing the position and the details of want he was going to do. I finished up with my philosophy on making mistakes.

"You are going to make errors," I said. "Do not worry about them-that is the only way you are going to learn."

When managing managers in multiple locations, I am always reluctant to spend a lot of time with new managers in their office; it creates an appearance that I am babysitting someone not yet competent enough to do the job. So I generally contented myself with one phone call to that manager every day.

But in Mark's case, I was besieged by phone calls from him almost immediately:

"Is it okay to sign this form?"

"Is okay if I spend money on this?"

After a week of spending my time making decisions he could easily have made for himself, I traveled over to his office to see what was going on. I was immediately accosted by several of his representatives.

"What did you give us?"

"What do you mean?" I responded.

"We need someone who can make a decision right away, and he has to wait for you on every decision. Doesn't he have management authority?"

Oops.

I sat down with Mark and asked him what was going on. "I am just not comfortable making these decisions until I have all the information I can get," he said.

I empathized with his situation; after all, he had spent a quarter century never making a decision on his own without management approval.

"The reason you are in management is so you can make these decisions right away," I said "I have eleven managers and 300 reps; I cannot make all those decisions for you.'

We spent some time walking about specific examples of where he could make decisions. Over the next several months, he started to become more independent. Sure, he made some mistakes, but I never overruled one of them. We talked about different ways he could improve his authority, but he was never comfortable with it.

Eventually, he went back into a bureaucratic job because he never felt comfortable taking responsibility for those decisions. I was happy he made that decision so that I did not need to make it for him.

What Is Innovation?

Innovation is the attempt to try something new in an effort to achieve a goal. The key word in that definition, of course, is *new*.

When you are faced with a situation or challenge, the last thing you want to do is reinforce the old ways of doing things. The reason the previous methods have failed is either they are no good, or times have changed to a point that the method is no longer useful.

In either case, you need to get a good, new idea on

how to solve your problem. If you cannot think of one, how are you going to get an idea?

Use Your Peers

Under the heading, "There are no new ideas, only borrowed ideas," a great source for getting innovative ideas is to question your peers.

As a senior manager, I got my managers and line supervisors together at least once per quarter for an off-site meeting. The only topic on the agenda was *innovation*.

At the meeting, each manager brought a list of three areas in which they had a challenge. It could be a difficult employee, or low production in a certain area, or office morale. The manager presented his/her problem, then each of the other managers indicated how they would handle the problem or — better yet — the other managers used their own similar experiences, and discussed how that challenge was solved.

In 1996, when I was still a line manager, I participated in a brainstorming session with my peers at a hotel near Santa Barbara. It was a relaxed atmosphere that contributed to the candor with which everyone spoke. At the time, my district was doing very well in all areas with the exception of one product line that did not generate much revenue for the company, nor did it generate much income for my reps. But achieving the annual goal in that product was essential.

I presented that sad saga to my peers, and ended up writing down eight ideas to increase production. We implemented four of them and made up my deficit and achieved the annual goal. I went back and thanked my colleagues for their advice, and each one shrugged it off; turns out each of them had received those brilliant ideas from someone else!

There is nothing wrong with obtaining ideas from other sources — if it works for them, it can work for you.

Use Your Team

Another good way of getting innovative ideas is from your team members. After all, they're the ones on the front line and know better than anyone how to fix things.

A couple of days prior to a team meeting, send an e-mail to your team reminding them of the meeting date and time. Also mention something like this:

> Our production in blue widgets this year is below goal. I have some ideas to correct this problem, but I would like each of you to think of a new idea we can put into practice to correct this.

Also encourage your team to come to you every time they have an idea. And make sure to find a way to make their idea work instead of immediately pooh-poohing it. You will gain respect. What is more, if you employ a team member's idea, they will be your best sales person when it comes to selling that idea to your whole team.

Managing Your B-Players

One thing I have learned since 2009, during the Great Recession, was that it's okay if not everyone on your team is a so-called A-player.

In the talent management world, a great deal is written

and discussed about the management of the A-players, the best employees, and those with the highest potential.

But what about the B-players?

First, it's ridiculous to conclude that your entire work-force is made up of (or should only include) A-players. There simply are not that many great employees to go around, and let's face it, not every company is Google or Patagonia with 1,500 applicants for every position. In the real world, you are going to have some B-players on your team.

Given the right direction and leadership, those employees have the capability of being extremely valuable to your organization. A Harvard Business Review study concluded that "companies' long-term performance — even survival — depends far more on the unsung commitment and contributions of their B players (than on A players)."

In my second book, *The Five A's of Great Employees*, I defined these so-called B-players as those with agility. Agility is really hard to train and develop. Employees must have a strong desire to play this role.

Let's use baseball as an analogy. The great teams have superstars — the .300 hitters with 40 homeruns. Those are your A-players. But teams that win the World Series invariably have several role players, sometimes called "utility" players. This is the player that will never hit 40 homers — but can play catcher, or right field, or second base. They are the ones that are able to sacrifice to advance base-runners, or break up double plays. They are the unsung heroes. And it's no coincidence they are sometimes called "character guys."

In the film industry—whether you are best supporting actor or best actor, the trophy is the same.

In the workplace, I would define B-players as those who:

- Show up for work every day, put their nose down, and grind out the work;

- Have little, if any drama associated with their presence in the workplace;

- Stay at your company for a longer than most employees;

- Use their abilities to the maximum;

- Consistently perform good but not spectacular work; and

- Often are defined by something other than work whether it be family or a significant hobby.

Give me a group of people like this, and I'll show you a very, very good workforce.

I have worked with a mid-sized CPA firm for a number of years, and I recall one such employee. Brad was very quiet (except at the company holiday party), showed up to work every day, and was incredibly reliable. Brad was well paid for a staff accountant, but because he was not spectacular, he never received significant promotions.

At corporate review meetings, the partners always wondered if they should let him go because he wasn't partner material.

My response to them was—not everyone is partner material! Not everyone has the capability of being a CEO! If you are under the impression that everybody in your workforce must have that potential, you are deluding yourself. Every workforce needs people to actually do the work, not just manage and lead.

The problem is, most managers and executives do not know how to manage B- players and as a result, those employees become disillusioned, lose their edge, or, worse, leave the company.

Here are some thoughts on how to manage B-players:

1. **Know Who They Are:** Your B-players are not mediocre or failing employees. Rather, they are hard workers who for reasons tangible or intangible are not going to be CEO someday.

2. **Manage them the same way you do your A-players:** That is, find out what their goals are, set your expectations clearly, and adapt a one-size-fits-one approach.

3. **Let them know their performance is valued:** If good employees see their superstar colleague get all the recognition and rewards, they're going to be disheartened.

4. **Make clear what their career path is:** If they are not ever going to be an executive or manager — let them know that. (It's not fair to them if they're laboring under the illusion that someday they will be promoted). There are other ways of rewarding performers than simply promotions.

5. **Pay them at the top of the market:** The value of the B-player is their stability to the company as well as consistent performance. If that employee leaves, it's going to be really expensive, and time consuming, to replace that person with a similar performer. It's

much less expensive to simply pay them at the top of the market.

I once worked with a commercial real estate firm that had the greatest receptionist I have ever seen. When she answered the phone, she did so as if she'd been waiting for your call all day long. Colleagues and competitors would constantly try to steal her every month. She had been in the position for eight or nine years when she decided to apply for a promotion within the company.

The owners knew that wasn't the best use of her skills and wanted to keep her in her role. Their answer? They raised her pay to twenty percent over what any other receptionist was making in town—and about ten to fifteen percent more than administrative assistants were being paid. She stayed. If she was going to leave, it wasn't going to be because of money.

Supporting actors have an increasingly critical role in business, but they won't flourish or remain without an intentional strategy for managing their performance and careers.

15

ADAPTING TO CHANGE

Change is one of the most misunderstood and feared actions in business. No one knows how to deal with it well. When things are going well, you do not want change. When things are going badly, change cannot happen fast enough.

To employees (including managers) the fear relating to change is simply the fear of the unknown. People get into comfort levels and resist mightily when someone or something attempts to break that comfort zone.

Regardless of whether it's good or bad change, it rests upon management's shoulders to incorporate the changes with a minimum of difficult.

Recently, a major change occurred in my company, one that would obviously result in lower production, which meant less commission for my sales managers and sales reps (and me, come to think of it). My boss asked me to evaluate the change prior to its announcement. I analyzed the change and made estimates on the production that would be lost, the commissions reduced and the emotional affect it would have on my team.

I presented my findings to my boss, who immediately

led me in to an executive meeting, where the top people in the company were sitting. They reviewed my memo and the senior executive threw it down and said, "I am not paying you to tell me what is going to go wrong; I've got analysts and product managers to do that. I want you to tell me how you are going to manage this situation to minimize the problems."

That was a bit harsh, but it re-opened my mind to what my responsibility was—to incorporate change with a minimum of difficulty. I spent the next few weeks figuring ways within my power that I could regain some of the lost business. When the change was finally announced, I was able to also announce several programs designed to increase other types of business

The Constancy of Change

No one likes change, yet change is the only constant there is. Because you are the leader, you are expected to both manage and lead change. So the first thing you must do is deal with it! You do not have any other option. You must absolutely accept change when it occurs because if you do not truly accept change your team will see through you like a window.

When change occurs, you do not have a choice. You must deal with it—so do so. Then foster that same attitude among your team. I have spent many years analyzing and studying all of the options you have when change occurs, whether you agree with the change or not. Following are all of those options:

1.   Deal with it
2.   Quit your job

That is it—those are truly the only options! Notice that complaining is not an option, being in a bad mood is not an option, and performing at a lower standard is not an option.

So, unless you want to quit your job, you have to find a way to deal with it.

Dealing with Change as a Manager

The first thing to do is find a way to make the change work for you and your team. What can you do within your power to mitigate the negative aspects of the change? How can you emphasize the positive aspects of change, if any?

Next, realize that you are a leader. You are on stage. Your team will know your nuances, so you are not allowed to show frustration or weakness in front of them. Leaders lead—they say "here is the way I believe we need to go," and then go. This is the attitude you must take when managing change.

In your professional life, you will always have to adapt to change. You will get a new job, there will be a new corporate change, and you will have different team members to deal with. The point I am making is that nothing stays the same, despite your most strenuous efforts to the contrary.

Before I started my own company, I had ten different jobs in thirteen different locations in seventeen years (granted, that is with only two companies, but it's still a lot). In a six-month period, I had a turnover in my sales force of thirty percent (more than fifty employees). That is substantial change.

The best way I know of dealing with change is a three-step process.

1. Accept it.
2. Embrace the best parts of it.
3. Change your focus.

Some people never accept change. They are the ones who have to leave or they become so jaded and negative they no longer are functioning members of your team. When change happens, it happens. End of story.

Virtually any change breeds opportunity — the key is *finding* the opportunity and acting on it. Focus on the positive.

Finally, any corporate change requires you to change. This isn't as complex as it sounds. You just have to change your focus. When corporate changes in my company results in a number of resignations, my focus — and that of my managers — changed from the management of reps to the recruiting and hiring of new reps.

One manager complained, "I am not a manager, I am a recruiter." I agreed with him.

"For the time being, a recruiter is exactly who you are," I told him. "We cannot move forward until we can get back to full staff. Nothing else matters until that happens."

For several months, up to fifty percent of my time and that of my managers was devoted to recruiting, interviewing, hiring, and training. When that period ended, we were able to change our focus back to other things.

16

Adding Value

A trend developed in the 1990s for salespeople. The MBAs and management consultants called it *value-add* or a similar term. At its core, a value-add was something that added value over and above the cost of an item or service. Nordstrom, for example, costs a lot more than Macy's. But people go to Nordstrom in droves because they perceive the value makes up for the additional cost.

Value is defined as benefits minus cost. Value is what you provide that makes the cost worth the money you paid.

It is far cheaper to send a package through the post office than via an overnight courier—but sometimes, the courier is worth the extra cost.

It is far cheaper to buy inexpensive vodka than premium vodka—but many people believe the premium vodka is worth it.

You can get a pair of pants for a lot less at Target than Bloomingdale's—but the quality of the product and service provided may make Bloomingdale's worth it.

As a manager, you can add value to your team the

same way a Nordstrom or Bloomingdale's add value to their product.

Employees today, as I mentioned earlier, crave value from the managers and supervisors.

What do you do that adds value to the professional lives of your team? And what can you do that add value to your team? Hopefully, many of the concepts and techniques mentioned in this book will help you in adding value.

As a newly transferred senior manager, I spent the first few weeks in my new position visiting my various offices getting to know the reps. In one office, I was shocked what the reps had to say about their manager, James. Some of the comments:

- "I do not know what he does all day."

- "He's a nice guy, but he's useless."

- "He doesn't do anything for us."

- "We'd be better off with no manager than him."

Obviously, my first priority became fixing that office. After spending time with the manager, it became evident to me that James was not practicing any basic management skills at all. James was indeed working, but he was mostly doing administrative work and did most of that away from the office. James was very good at talking at his team, and all of them consequently thought he was a nice guy, but not a good manager.

I started by asking James some personal questions about his reps: "Where does she live? Is he married?" James was unable to answer any of those questions, even though he had worked with this team for over a year. Turns out I knew more about his team that he did.

Then, I went to more penetrating questions: "When was the last time you had a one-on-one business review with your reps?"

His answer: "Uh ... a long time."

"How recently did you ask your team what they wanted from you?"

"Um, I do not remember actually doing that before."

What James failed to do was exactly what his team wanted his to do—find out their needs, and then deliver on his promises. James was working, but he was not working for his team. And his team was not performing for him.

A great lesson in adding value is that your team will do for you in direct proportion to what you do for them.

How You Can Add Value

The first step in adding value is performing a needs analysis. That is a fancy term for asking the members of your team what you need them to do. It's as simple as, "What do you need from me to make you more successful?"

The answers may surprise you and will always vary by individual. Some people need a manager to help expedite processing problems, or to function as an ear for their personal concerns. Others will need additional training or support.

It is pretty simple after that—find out what they need from you, and make sure to do it for them. Do not delegate this to someone else unless you absolutely have to. It is critical that they see you doing it. They are asking you for help because they do not feel they can get that help from anyone else.

So, as you periodically evaluate yourself as a manager, two of the first questions you should ask of yourself are:

✓ "Am I adding value to my team?"

✓ "Is my team better off, more successful and happier because I am here?"

If you cannot answer these questions, make sure to ask your team and request their full honesty. Feedback — candid feedback — is crucial to your success in adding value as a manager.

17

Committing To Your Success

When you get a moment, take a step back and look at your team. Which ones are committed and which are not? Do the same thing with your peers and your bosses.

I will bet it is easier than you think to identify who is committed and who is not.

Employees and managers, who are truly committed work harder, show more evidence of success and display a desire to win that isn't around those who are not committed.

You can never be successful unless you fully commit to your success and those of your team. That means you do not have doubts about where you are working, what you are doing or whom you are doing it for. Commitment means you are thrilled to be doing what you are doing; you do not have a second career and you do not have a half-written novel in your desk drawer.

Pure and honest commitment means you have vowed to so whatever it takes in order to succeed. And you won't stop until you've succeeded.

Take a look at pro golfer Tiger Woods, who completed the Grand Slam of Golf earlier than anyone in history. At just 24 he was — by a drive and a 3-wood — the best golfer in the world. His talent and prodigious drives are truly awesome. But what impresses most golfers the most is his commitment to his game. No one practices more or works harder on his game than Tiger. Many golfers practice chipping out of the rough; they place the ball in the rough and hit the ball. Not Tiger. He steps on the ball, giving it the worst possible lie and then spends an hour hitting those balls. And when the time comes for him to hit a ball in that lie in a tournament, he's prepared. Woods' commitment to success is sincere and obvious to all around him.

What is especially compelling about his story is his success following major back surgeries and personal problems. His determination after these adversities, led him to win The Masters at age 43 and lead his team to a President's Cup win in 2018.

The best thing about commitment is that it's an *acquired* trait and not inherited. Anyone with desire can make a commitment. Always give me someone with a desire and commitment to succeed than someone who has better credentials but does not have the commitment. It's impossible to imbue someone with desire. Either you want to or you do not. It is that simple.

When a former company I worked for opened a new office in a new location, it was a prototype office — something the company had never done before — offering new services and not offering traditional ones. The whole company was focused on the success of the office — the CEO was asking about it constantly.

In staffing the office, the most important decision I had was who the supervisor would be. Six long-time employees applied, and this would be a solid promotion for each of them. Five of the employees had substantial experience in the areas we were looking for and had solid backgrounds as well.

Yet, I hired the sixth candidate—an employee with fourteen years in the company, but only a few years of experience in our specific industry. She clearly had the most enthusiasm and passion and therefore would make a commitment in her heart to the job that no one else could. Why was that important? Because in a critical, visible position like that, I needed someone who could quickly adapt to change, roll with the punches, deal with a great deal of pressure and react to the unforeseen problems that always occur when a new project or office is launched.

And she succeeded, as I knew she would. The lesson is that commitment and passion are better predictors of future success than any résumé can provide. Her enthusiasm allowed her to learn and gain more experience faster than someone with theoretically stronger credentials.

If you truly want to succeed, first make the commitment in your mind. Nothing less than full success will do.

Become a Student of Successful People

Spend time with your peers who are successful and whom you admire. What do they do that works? You have to eliminate pride. There are always people who do well, and there is nothing wrong with finding out what their keys to success are.

One of my finest managers—Ann—was a young lady with a good mind, rooted with sound business sense and solid street smarts. She came from a moneyed family, which ordinarily would mean she did not have to work hard to have a comfortable lifestyle. But Ann had something to prove — to herself, to her family, and to a boss (not me) who did not promote her the first time she applied for management.

But when she was finally promoted, she took off. No one worked harder than Ann did — I am talking eighty to ninety hours a week. She micromanaged all of her reps and developed new training seminars to increase sales. She aggressively worked outside fairs and sporting events to sell products. But most of all, she demanded no less of her reps than she demanded of herself. It became natural for her reps to put in extra hours because Ann was there. Half of her team was there on Saturday mornings because Ann was there. Nowhere else in the organization was this dedication and commitment so evident.

Within weeks, her team — one of the greenest and underachieving teams in the company — became highly successful. Ann soon became the highest paid sales manager in the company. Her reps earned more than reps anywhere else. Reps in other offices begged to get on Ann's team.

Instead of finding out what Ann was doing to be so successful, her peers became jealous. According to her peers, her success was due to "favoritism' (from me) and more favorable working conditions than anywhere else. I ended up having each of my other managers spend an entire week with Ann — five fourteen- or fifteen-hour days, plus Saturday and Sunday — so they could see for themselves what commitment was all about.

Do not become jealous of someone's success; become his or her student. An organization becomes successful when everyone succeeds. One of my fellow senior managers said it best.

He said, "I want all of our regions to make their

goals—then, I want to be a little bit better than anyone else."

Do not root for someone to fail. It's better when we all succeed, and you put your ego in your back pocket and learn from success.

Learn Self-Discipline

For me, self-discipline is the hardest task to learn. Yet self-discipline is critical if you are to fully commit to your success. It took me a lot of years to really understand it. Running my own business is what really turned the tide because for many years it was "if not me, who?" (Today, I have a team that has made that issue infinitely easier for me.)

An executive whom I have worked with closely over the years, and whom I admire greatly, defines self-discipline this way: *Self-discipline is doing what needs to be done, when it needs to be done, whether you feel like it or not.*

Self-discipline is about the commitment you make to yourself and your team. It's about following through on your promises to yourself, your boss, and your team. Self-discipline is doing what you said you would do.

The heart of self-discipline is self-respect. You must have enough respect for yourself, your values and your talent to constantly commit to the promises you make. There is no way to get self-discipline without self-respect.

Abraham Heschel once said, "Self-respect is the fruit of discipline: the sense of dignity grows with the ability to say no to oneself."

The part of management I despise the most is terminating employees. Eventually, all managers have to do it; there is no avoiding this problem.

When it was time to terminate an employee, I would find any reason I could to delay the process. I would invent meetings, or get too late of a start on my drive, or decide the next day was a better day to do it.

Actually, what I was doing was a disservice to that employee. I needed to get it over with faster — for both my benefit and that of the person about to be terminated. When I was in doubt whether to pull the trigger, I would imagine myself going home and going to bed with the nagging problem ahead of me — I have to fire someone tomorrow. I would sit in my office and think, "Do I really want this hanging over my head for another day and night, or do I just want to get this over with?"

That is a fairly selfish attitude to be sure, but one that motivated me to get the job done sooner rather than later.

Following Through On Your Commitments

A frequent complaint I hear from employees is, "My manager said he/she was going to do (something) and then never did."

A key to your success is to be able to follow through on the commitments you make — to anyone, actually, but in this case I am referring to your team.

If you say you are going to do something, you have no alternative but to do it, and the sooner, the better. The fastest way to lose respect is not to follow through on a commitment.

Think of it this way: if your boss asks you to do something, do not you take every step possible to make sure it gets done promptly? You should feel the same way when an employee asks you to do something.

I tend to judge people not by the way they treat their superiors or their peers, but by the way they treat their subordinates, or a waiter in a restaurant. Successful people treat everyone with equal respect, and successful managers treat requests from their team with the same priority and verve they handle orders from their boss.

18

PLANNING TO SUCCEED

In previous chapters, we have talked about the need to develop action plans and expectations for your team. A list of goals and a road map are critical for success.

Thus, you must have a plan to win. This plan cannot be reactive; you must be pro-active. And once the plan is in place, everything else is scrap. Any good time management consultant will tell you scrap is the anathema of success.

When you establish and set goals and expectations, and you have a plan for winning that you believe in, never let anything else get in your way.

A good idea is to create an annual theme. At both companies I worked for, we had a deluxe trip for the top sales people. The top salespeople and managers and their guests would fly to a location like Hawaii or Tahiti and stay in five-diamond hotels for several days. That made it easy to create a theme.

When a new vice-president took over my division in the mid-1990s, he made sure that everyone knew his annual theme. He would have an annual "State of the Union" speech where he would launch his theme, and then recount it through the year. When he sent an e-mail, his e-mail signature would include the theme. This is a helpful tool to keep your plan and your ultimate goal in front of your team throughout the year.

Cut to the Chase

There are better time managers than I am. Just ask any assistant who has worked with me! But even I know that efficiency is the key to your plan and improving your plan to succeed. Remember: the most efficient way to get where you want to go is a straight line! Do not deviate from the line. Most managers can easily be diverted into issues that do not get you where you need to go. Do not be one of these managers! It's your job to point the team in the right direction and keep them going in that direction.

A friend of mine understands "The Big Picture" better than anyone I know. Stan is co-owner of a company that owns and manages tens of thousands of apartment and business rentals throughout Southern California. I have great respect for his business acumen, but even more respect for how quickly he grasps the heart of an issue. When I sit with him on committees, or consult with him on my managerial problems, he always focuses on "The Big Picture." When a mutual friend became president of a prestigious organization, I sat with Stan and the new president and listened as Stan gave his best advice:

- *Think Big Thoughts*
- Write Them Down
- Take a Balanced Approach

- Plan to Succeed

- Have A Purpose

Be Specific

These are excellent point for any executive or manager to remember. If you live by these ideals, and can communicate them with authority, your success will be easy to come by.

19

KEY CHARACTERISTICS OF OUTSTANDING MANAGERS

I've spent most of this book talking about methods you can learn to become a great manager. Obviously, there are people who possess innate personal characteristics that help them naturally succeed. I've spent many years watching and learning from many of them, and I'll share with you now the key characteristics they possess that haven't been learned, but are ingrained in their personality nonetheless.

Outstanding managers innately possess:

1. The desire to win
2. The ability to adapt to change
3. An open mind
4. No pre-conceived notions
5. Vision
6. Leadership
7. The ability to treat everyone fairly and consistently
8. The ability to honestly self-evaluate each day
9. World class communications skills

Do you have each of these characteristics? I certainly do not, but I try as hard as possible to live up to these ideals in my every day life.

Two Keys to Understanding Success

1. The world is a mirror
2. You become what you think about

One of my favorite and best-received speeches is a presentation simply called "The Mirror." It's a program designed to focus attention on the one person in the world you can motivate you — the person you see in the mirror.

And the world is a mirror. It's your mirror. No one else can get you to do what you want to do.

What an empowering thought! It's also a scary thought: your success rests entirely upon your shoulders.

Winners want that burden. They encourage it. Michael Jordan always wanted the ball at the end of the game. Winners always want to take the last shot.

I have played competitive sports all my life, and I have been in dozens of last-second situations. None could compare to the moment twenty years ago when I was the captain of my four-person paddle tennis team in a huge tournament. When the championship match went to a tiebreak format, only two players could be drawn to complete. Two of my teammates were selected at random, and not me.

I had to sit on the sidelines and watch, helplessly, as my teammates played in the tiebreaker. I was incredibly nervous watching them, and I never had that feeling when I was on the court — only when matters were taken out of my hands. It's an awful feeling. I want to be the one at crunch time, the one who makes the big decision. If you want this as well, you are a winner.

Never be afraid to fail. Be afraid of not trying.

Winning Is Habitual

When I first started in sales, all of the experienced reps and my management team spent hours working with me on attaining my goals for the quarter and the year. Those reps that achieved annual goals were sent on a wonderful trip — usually Hawaii. What these people told me was the same: "Once you go on this trip, you will do anything you can to go every year."

And it's true! The same people who went to the trip one year were there every year — they found a way to succeed, and winning then became habitual.

In 1998, I was planning yet another promotion for our reps. I tried to have five or six promotions and contests a year, in addition to the corporate competitions. I finished the proposal and, after reviewing it, my boss called me in.

After a few preliminary questions, he got right to his big concern: "I am tired of seeing the same people win all of these contests. What guarantee do you have that some new people are going to be here?"

I was really surprised, and went back to review previous promotions. And he was right. No matter what the reward (trip, cash, luncheons, or dinners) or the contest — whether it was for top production or quality service or teamwork — the same people always ended up winning.

One rep told me, "I just like to win. It doesn't matter what the carrot is. I like to know for myself that I can do it."

Everywhere I have been, there are always a group of reps and managers who reliably will achieve all of their goals. Those are the winners—the ones who know how to win and have made a habit of it.

Only the carrot motivates other people. For example, many salespeople love cash. If there is a sufficient cash incentive for a contest, people unaccustomed to winning will make an effort to achieve. Those are not the people I am referring to. We are looking for the people who are there every day, of every week of every year, committed to success. So is your boss. So should you.

Eric's Philosophies of Leadership

Based on these characteristics of outstanding managers, I have created several philosophies of leadership that I use when managing teams (and when training others to manage teams).

Philosophy Number One: *Most people get promoted to management for reasons that have nothing to do with their ability to lead people.*

- ✓ They sell the most widgets; or
- ✓ They're the hardest worker; or
- ✓ They kiss the most ass; or
- ✓ They've been there the longest; or
- ✓ In government, you even have to pass a written examination to get promoted.

Philosophy Number Two: *Leadership can be learned.*

As we discussed earlier in this section, some people have innate characteristics that make them great leaders. However, as suggested by Philosophy Number One, people lacking those innate characteristics are oftentimes promoted.

The good news is that these people can learn to be leaders. However, learning must be desired, and it must be ongoing.

Philosophy Number Three: *Great leaders must be values-articulate.*

Before anything else, an effective leader must be able to articulate his/her core values and expectations of themselves, the people they work for and with, and the people who work for them. Understanding and living your values makes every decision you make easier.

Philosophy Number Four: *Therefore, who you are is how you lead.*

Philosophy Number Five: *Communication is king.*

The ability to effectively communicate supersedes any other important leadership tenet. You can be the smartest person in the room, the most dedicated person, or achieve success in other areas, but unless you can communicate well, you are never going to succeed in leadership.

Philosophy Number Six: *Hire for what you cannot teach.*

Whereas most people hire based on ability, great leaders

hire for attitude, aptitude, alignment, and agility. Ability can be taught; attitude, aptitude, alignment, and agility cannot be.

Philosophy Number Seven: *Give credit freely to others.*

After thirty years in leadership, I can say without hesitation what goes around comes around. Maybe not immediately, but ultimately.

Philosophy Number Eight: *Treat every person as though you'll be working for them one day.*

It's happened to me.

Philosophy Number Nine: *Always be learning.*

In leadership development, there is no end zone. The workforce is moving too fast for any leader to stay stagnant. Lack of learning and curiosity will make you irrelevant faster than any other mistake you can make.

Philosophy Number Ten: *You can learn just as much from bad bosses as good bosses.*

Remember the qualities of the best boss you've ever had and make sure you exemplify those qualities every day.

Philosophy Number Eleven: *A great measure of good leadership is how things run when you are not there.*

Philosophy Number Twelve: *Great leaders are crystal clear about their weaknesses.*

They have no illusions and are totally transparent about what their weaknesses are. They hire people who emphasize their strengths and compensate for their weaknesses.

APPENDIX

WHAT TO DO WHEN YOU GET THERE

What You Need to Do the First Day You Are There

1. Be the first one in the office.
2. E-mail your team with your schedule for the upcoming week. (And call them "your team.")
3. Walk around and introduce yourself to everyone on your team (or personally say hello to them if you've already met them).

    a. If any of them have a concern or issue, make sure to resolve it TODAY.
    b. Make sure to let them know how excited you are to be there.
    c. Ask your team if they prefer morning or evening meetings.

4. Have your peer managers introduce you to their teams.
5. Take your assistant, if you have one, out to lunch.
6. Repeat with your second office, if you have multiple offices.

7. Be the last one to leave your office.

What You Need to Do the First Week You Are There

    a. Recognize and reward the top performers.
- If you do not have a lot of top performers, invent a category that someone has succeeded in.
- Create wins.
- Find a reason to praise people.

    b. Set your expectations:
- What you expect from your team.
- What they can expect from you.
- What your goals are for the team in the coming year.
- Your "pet peeves."
- Get the numbers:
  1) Where they have been.
  2) Where you are going.

    c. Establish a regular monthly team meeting date and time (for example, the first Friday morning of each month).

    d. Establish dates for one-on-one business reviews.

1. Identify one person in each office that has the potential for doing better, sit down with them right away, let them know they have that potential, and tell them how you can help them get there.

2. Identify the leaders in the office and get them on your side by asking their future goals. If it includes management, tell them you will help them get there and make sure to follow up on it!

What You Need to Do the Second Week You Are There

1. Conduct one-on-one meetings with each person on your team for thirty minutes each.

    a. First Question: "What do you need from me?"
    b. Solicit their opinion of their performance and review.
    c. Discuss their career path.
        -   If they're in sales, how can you help them get to their earnings goal?
        -   Ask: "What is your career goal?"
            1) Identify career goal for five years.
            2) Identify career goal for the long-term.
            3) Identify how you can help them get to their career goal.
    d. Identify needs, such as:
        -   Marketing support.
        -   Underwriting help.
        -   More leads.
        -   Better time management.
2. Sit with each of your team member for twenty minutes.

    a. Observe their interaction with their peers and clients.
    b. Offer suggestions for improvement.
    c. Ask them, "How would you run this office?"

What You Need to Do the Third Week You Are There

1. Deliver on the needs identified last week.
2. Take the leaders in the office out to lunch.

a. Tell them you are counting on them to lead and explain why it's so important they do so.
b. Offer them incentives for their leadership.
3. Work with the front lines with your team, doing their jobs with them.
    - This establishes your credibility.

What You Need to Do the Fourth Week You Are There

1. Complete a comprehensive business plan for your team and review it with your boss.

    a. After revisions are made, present it to your team during a business meeting.
    b. Get buy-in from the team on the different areas of your plan.

Things to Do Each and Every Week

1. Be the first one in the office at least twice a week.
2. Be the last one in the office at least once a week.
3. Always remember you are always on stage.
4. Always remember you cannot expect more from your team than you do from yourself — if you want them to work hard, you have to work harder.
5. It is not about the hours you put in but the results you get.
6. If you have a sales team, identify your underperformers and meet with them once per week.

    a. Tell them: "I am going to help you make more money than you ever have before."
7. Totally commit to the job. It is not 9-5. It is how many hours it takes to succeed.

Acknowledgments

Original Acknowledgements, 2003

There are few good original ideas; mostly just good ideas we've learned from others and adopted as our own.

The concept behind this book is to discuss what I've learned in almost twenty years in sales, training, and management. Many lessons are those I havelearned on my own, by making good and bad decisions and learning from them. The vast majority of thoughts in this book, however, are those I've learned from others. Working with other managers who were my superiors, my peers or my friends truly formed the core of my management beliefs and theories.

This is not a scholarly work, based on years of detailed research. Instead, this book is about the lessons I have learned by actually being there in the trenches. One of my beliefs is that the most valuable lessons you learn are from observing other managers in action. You do not need a professional speaker or a college professor telling you how to manage; you need to watch others. Find people whom you respect and watch them in action, in meetings and in repose and you will learn more over a period of time than in any management class. That is what I did.

I am extraordinarily grateful, therefore, to the following managers and leaders from whom I've learned so much. Many of their actions and theories are in this book.

In that vein, I wish to thank Robert Bouttier, George Clarke, Chris Hans, Michael O'Steen, Sharon Neiman and Tiffany Perrucci. I never worked for Dave Jones, but I was privileged to work with him in a variety of capacities and learned management lessons — both in quantity and quality — from him every day.

I am also grateful to Rocco Muratore, Steve Hanson, Ted Haase, and Jack van Etten for their wisdom and experience. And friends like Jay Eagan and Greg Hickey have spent a great deal of time with me on a personal level, giving advice from their own professional and personal experiences.

I wish to thank Kirsten Hansen for her wonderful, critical eye in reading and reviewing the numerous drafts of this book and her varying levels of patience in tolerating me over the years.

Finally, I wish to thank my parents for their faith.

Eric Swenson
November, 2003
Los Angeles, California

Author's Updates, 2020

I re-read my 2003 acknowledgements with a fairly sentimental eye. A few people are no longer with us, and I have lost track of some of the people I mentioned. That happens: when you leave one company for another, you might promise to stay in touch, but it never really happens that way. On the other hand, two friends I mentioned in 2003—Jay Eagan and Greg Hickey—are still close. They were part of my wedding in 2010, and the three of us had dinner just last week.

I left AAA in 2001, years before LinkedIn and other social media made it much easier to keep track of long-lost comrades. It's been easier to track my former colleagues from Paychex, because we actually are all on LinkedIn.

Since I wrote this book in 2003, so much in my life has changed. Instead of learning leadership from my bosses in a corporate culture, I have been learning and observing the workforce and leadership from the hundreds of businesses and thousands of leaders who have been clients since 2004.

My business has grown, as has the number of clients, the services we offer, and what we do. But I do not have much of a sense of accomplishment as I do of gratitude. No one succeeds on their own. I have an amazing team at RSJ/Swenson. I had a rare flash of brilliance to hire Jamie Baker in 2010. She leads our team with grace, effectiveness, and calm. I am constantly in a state of gratitude for her and our team.

I'll never be able to adequately thank people in my circle—whether employees, partners, clients, referral sources, vendors, or friends (many of whom are a combination of these). I couldn't reach any level of success without you.

My best clients are those from whom I learn as much as I teach, where owners/CEOs want to do the right thing because it's the right thing to do, not because it is the cheapest or most expedient way to do it.

I am hesitant to name everyone because I know I am going to forget someone, but I want to name names, so if I forgot you, my profound apologies. Either that, or I did not think you were all that! (Just kidding, Tony.)

I will start with the leaders I work with whom I greatly admire. Most, if not all, of these people are not just clients but also friends, and whom the give-and-take is mutual and impactful: James Dal Pozzo, Dada Ngo, Steve Brown, Patrick Miller, Ross Resnick (my frient), Ranlyn Hill, Larry Scherzer, Chris Lewis, Michael Shanklin, Megan Watanabe, Rabbi Yoshi Zweiback, Herb Smith, and Melissa Cerny.

There are a number of people who I interact with—whether as an advisor for their clients or themselves. They are highly successful and have allowed me into their personal and/or professional lives as a trusted advisor. The best part of being a trusted advisor is I get twice as much as I give. I never take them for granted and indeed and extraordinarily grateful I am part of their lives: Steve Fishman, Glenn Sonnenberg, Robert Blumenfield, Sharon Spira-Cushnir, Sophia Harang, Farah Ansari, Randy Moore, and Michael Blacher.

When I give speeches or offer client advice, or want to know more about how to be the best professional I can be, I turn to my "workforce heroes." Each has a sizeable library on their websites and social media accounts. Each month, I review their websites, writing, and social media posts. I would recommend any of them as the premier experts of contemporary workforce and leadership thought. I admire each of them, and have met none of them! They include: Professor Adam Grant, Laszlo Bock, Professor Laura Huang, Shawn Achor, Simon Sinek, Jonas Prising, Brené Brown, and Marcus Buckingham.

Dan Sullivan and his program, "Strategic Coach," has had more influence on my success as an entrepreneur than any single person ever. Many thousands have been influenced by his concepts; I have been transformed by them. There are few true geniuses in the world; he is one of them. And sincere appreciation to Colleen Bowler and Valentine Chavez-Gonzalez for tolerating an unreasonable amount of questions, my self-doubts, and the rants of the newly converted (me).

Tony Rose and Jake Jacobs brought me into their fold and stuck by me during some extraordinarily difficult times in 2009 and lasting through 2011. The quality I admire most in our fellow humans is loyalty, and I am glad to have the opportunity to repay their faith in me. (The quality I despise most in our fellow humans? Hypocrisy, a quality neither Tony nor Jake has ever shown.)

My next book is called *Weaknesses*, which calls for everyone to embrace their failings, not ignore them. Instead of wasting time trying to get better, bring people around them who are masters of those areas that are your weaknesses.

One of my (many) weaknesses is finance. I never got it and years ago gave up trying to master it.

In 2009, at the depth of the Great Recession, I did not have very many professional friends. A 29-year-old accountant named Shana Merrill came into my office one day and took the time to explain (my bleak) financial report to me in a way I finally understood. I asked her why she was being so nice to me.

She said, "It's because I am the only one here who understands that you are not an accountant."

And so, for the past eleven years, my closest professional friend (yes, I said professional friend) has been Shana. It is an extraordinary gift to be around someone every day in business who is so different from you, yet who completely gets you. Our biggest disagreement is who gets more out of our conversations. I'll call it a tie. Gratefully.

And speaking of gratitude: my greatest win and success in life—without question - was getting my wife to marry me in 2010. Yukiji has been equal parts motivator, great expectations setter, honest critic, and advocate. It has been a wonderful ride, and that ride after ten years continues to get better and better, thanks to you. I am lucky, fortunate, grateful, and humbled to have you as my partner in life.

Eric Swenson
January 1, 2020
Westwood, California

About the Author

Workforce strategist, author, and speaker: Eric Swenson is acknowledged as a leading expert on management and leadership. His work with businesses throughout North America has led to improved performance, stronger employee engagement, and greater customer satisfaction.

He has conducted his cutting edge leadership development programs before thousands of senior executives and managers, as well as first time supervisors.

Eric has written two books: *Managing People in the 21st Century* and *The 5 A's of Great Employees*, the latter of which became a best-selling book in 2016.

A sought-after speaker, he speaks frequently to organizations and conferences on topics ranging from leadership and management, to workforce trends and issues. He has conducted seminars for professional organizations and is a popular keynote speaker at conferences and conventions.

Eric is the founder and managing director of RSJ/Swenson, a human resources and workforce outsourcing firm serving more than 300 businesses in North America. Those businesses range from start-ups to established companies with over 1,000 employees. Virtually every industry is represented in RSJ/Swenson's portfolio.

Eric founded his firm in 2003 and merged it with the CPA firm of Rose, Snyder & Jacobs in 2008.

He has managed hundreds of employees and interviewed thousands of job candidates in his career.

Prior to launching RSJ/Swenson, he led the HR outsourcing division in Southern California for Paychex, a Fortune 1000 company providing payroll and human resources solutions to small businesses.

He also spent fourteen years with the Automobile Club of Southern California, having advanced from sales agent to senior management. Also at the Auto Club, Eric spent several years in marketing and training, where he first gained his initial interest in leadership development.

Eric was born in Los Angeles and grew up in Arcadia, California. An Eagle Scout, he is a graduate of the University of the Pacific, where he majored in English and communications and was student body president at the College of the Pacific.

He's currently developing groundbreaking new talent and leadership programs that focus on contemporary, practical solutions to today's contemporary workforce issues.

He and his wife, Yukiji, live in Los Angeles.

Visit his websites:
www.ericwswenson.com
www.tanzaniteleadership.com
www.rsjswenson.com

CPSIA information can be obtained
at www.ICGtesting.com
Printed in the USA
FSHW011117220720
71818FS

9 781627 877923